Histories of Community-Based Art Education

by

Kristin G. Congdon
Doug Blandy
Paul E. Bolin

National Art Education Association

D1513082

About the National Art Education Association

The National Art Education Association is the world's largest professional art education association and a leader in educational research, policy, and practice for art education. NAEA's mission is to advance art education through professional development, service, advancement of knowledge, and leadership.

Membership (approximately 40,000) includes elementary and secondary art teachers (and middle and senior high students in the National Art Honor Society programs), artists, administrators, museum educators, arts council staff, and university professors from throughout the United States and several foreign countries. It also includes publishers, manufacturers and suppliers of art materials, parents, students, retired art educators, and others concerned about quality art education in our schools.

The Association publishes several journals, papers, and flyers on art education; holds an annual convention; conducts research; sponsors a teacher awards program; develops standards on student learning, school programs and teacher preparation; and cosponsors workshops, seminars and institutes on art education. For further information, contact our web site at www.naea-reston.org.

© 2001 National Art Education Association
1916 Association Drive
Reston, VA 20191

Order No. 280
ISBN 1-890160-08-3

Table of Contents

To the next generation of storytellers

We would like to thank many people who have helped to make this anthology possible. Eldon Katter and Thomas A. Hatfield from the National Art Education Association (NAEA) saw the need for a second volume of histories that had not yet been told. Paddy Bowman, Coordinator of the National Task Force on Folk Arts in Education enthusiastically partnered in this second volume, as she did *in Remembering Others: Making Invisible Histories of Art Education Visible*. Patrica Stuhr and Christine Ballengee Morris co-chairs of the National Art Education Association's Research Task Force on Context have our gratitude for their belief in a second publication on this topic. We had clerical help from Deborah Snider and a variety of suggestions and support from students at the University of Central Florida, the University of Oregon, and The Pennsylvania State University. And, as always, we thank our respective families for their patience and assistance.

Histories of Community-Based Art Education

Introduction

In 1998 we issued a call for manuscripts for a National Art Education Association (NAEA) anthology on "invisible" histories of art education. In response we received an astonishing one hundred chapter proposals. Twenty-one were developed into chapters and testimonials for *Remembering Others: Making Invisible Histories of Art Education Visible* (Bolin, Congdon, & Blandy, 2000). Divided into three sections, this first volume includes chapters on formal education settings; community arts and museum settings; and folk groups.

Because of the large and unexpected number of proposals received, the NAEA invited us to edit this second volume. This anthology concentrates on histories of community-based art education. Like the first volume, *Histories of Community-Based Art Education* brings to the fore stories, experiences, teaching methods, and cultural groups whose histories have not been fully explored, documented, or appreciated. This second anthology, like the first, is a joint effort of the NAEA, the NAEA Research Commission Task Force on Contexts, and the National Task Force on Folk Arts in Education. Its content reflects recent changes in historical writing that include a broadening of what is considered worthy of historical study, moving beyond the study of written documents, a receptivity to multiple responses to historical questions, and an acknowledgment of the subjectivity of historical writing (Burke, 1991).

Many of the histories included in this anthology have not been adequately, or previously, documented in print. They have existed

primarily through stories told among family members, in neighborhoods, cultural organizations, special interest groups, ethnic groupings,
and at professional meetings. We chose many of the chapters for this
anthology because of their author's use of oral history. This editorial
strategy demonstrates our belief in the importance of art education
history that is representative of many and varied points of view. As
one elderly Nookta woman said: "Kill a memorizer and you kill a
whole hunk'a history, and if your're gonna kill someone's history,
well, your own might not last long, and when that's gone, you just
killed all your people who were here before you, all over again"
(Nookta woman cited in Cameron, 1981, p. 78).

Oral history, as remembered truth, differs from written narratives
because it continually exists in the present and is often reshaped
(unlike the printed word) and made flexible to accommodate the
present (Lowenthal, 1985). This fluid and semi-simultaneous perspective contributes to the understanding of the past as ever present and
relevant. The past is witnessed and appreciated in today's practices. It
is also important to note that in oral history facts are less important
than the reputation and credibility of the storyteller. We are pleased
that many chapters in this anthology incorporate this kind of integra-
tive interpretation of art education, where a relative or family member
is viewed as a historian.

Our concentration on community-based art education history in this
second volume is also motivated by an absence of a comprehensive
history of community-based arts initiatives in the United States.
Currently there is no consensus on when such a history begins.
Goldbard (1993) posits that what we now think of as community arts
began in the 1960s with programs like the San Francisco Neighborhood Arts Program (NAP). Dreeszen (1994) sees a much longer
historical trajectory. His history begins with the inception of the
Village Improvement Movement in 1853 through the City Beautiful
Movement (1893), Outdoor Art Movement (1899), Community
Theatre Movement (1915), Cooperative Extension Service (1937),
Works Progress Administration (1933), Civil Rights Movement
(1960s), Comprehensive Employment Training Act (CETA) (1970s),
to the present day. While Goldbard and Dreeszen's contributions to
the history of community arts are important for providing points of

reference and areas of debate, detailed studies of events, programs, people, purposes, and places are needed to support, supplement, and elaborate their points-of-view toward a comprehensive historical perspective.

The contributors to *Histories of Community-Based Art Education* affirm that the history of community-based art education and community arts is associated with people coming together in local arts centers, museums, schools, religious facilities, social clubs, recreation facilities, and civic associations among other settings, both formal and informal. Viewed from this perspective, art education incorporates a broad range of art objects and practices. This includes the traditional and popular arts. These diverse art objects and practices function, in part, as catalysts for dialogue about individual and group identity, local and national concerns, and ultimately the pursuit of democracy. Contributors to this anthology encourage an understanding of the richness, diversity, and complexity associated with community-based art education within democracy and civil society.

Civil society has as its purpose the facilitation of, "space for public discourse, for the development of public values and public language, for the formation of the public self [the citizen], a space separate from the formal political sphere dominated by the state power and political parties that aim to control that power" (Lummis, 1996, p. 31). The pursuit of democracy and civil society is a project that requires a life long commitment exercised within multiple and diverse venues. West (1999) reminds us that the "roots of democracy are fundamentally grounded in mutual respect, personal responsibility, and social accountability" (p. 10). Community-based arts education settings have been, and continue to be, among those informal and formal enclaves in which people assemble, work, and act together for a variety of political, cultural, economic, and educational purposes. These purposes are ultimately directed towards debating and creating the common good. In this regard, art education that is community-based has the potential to encourage "good" citizenship. Good citizens are those "who make a life commitment to maintaining and sharing with other fellow citizens those material conditions that enable political participation" (Batstone & Mendieta, 1999, p. 2). Good citizens also stand for "autonomy, self-legislation, and sense of civic solidarity that members of a group extend to one another" (Batstone & Mendieta, 1999, p. 3).

Fostering civil society requires constant vigilance and cultivation. As a society we are currently witnessing some disturbing trends that affirm the importance of such vigilance and cultivation. Putnam (1995) includes among such trends voter apathy and a drop in attendance at public meetings. Many of the chapters in this book illustrate successes at creating spaces and programs that bring people together and then engage them in the arts as a part of the discourse required by democracy and that nourishes civil society. Research confirms that communities with a lively and engaged constituency are more likely to successfully identify and solve problems of mutual concern (Putnam, 1995). Civic health can be measured by people's participation in the community (Shudson, 1999).

Contributors to *Histories of Community-Based Art Education* confirm personal and communal identity as they describe aesthetic orientations, problem-solving approaches, and ways of living. Traditions of the past are re-created in the present. Documenting this process in print encourages our understanding and appreciation of how this happens and enables us to make choices about who we are and who we want to become. Authors also document community-based arts initiatives that encourage and model civic engagement in a variety of ways involving diverse participants and myriad venues. Over time such initiatives have fostered the coordination and communication of discussions associated with important social issues. They have encouraged people to act collectively on matters of mutual concern. At times they have provided a "free space" in which people learn to articulate what they believe in, appreciate the power of collective action, and find support for their struggle to bring about positive social change.

Ultimately, as editors, we concur with Berger's (1972) belief that a narrowly interpreted history usually serves an elite and is unjustifiable and nonsensical in modern times (p. 11). We are grateful to the contributors' important work in providing an expanded view or our past and present by giving voice to histories that have not been previously well documented or even documented at all.

Kristin G. Congdon, Doug Blandy, and Paul E. Bolin, Editors

References

Batstone, D., & Mendieta, E. (1999). What does it mean to be an American? In D. Batstone, & E. Mendieta (Eds.), *The good citizen* (pp. 1-4). New York: Routledge.

Berger, J. (1972). *Ways of seeing*. London: Penguin.

Bolin, P., Congdon, K. G., & Blandy, D. (Eds.). (2000). *Remembering others: Making invisible histories of art education visible*. Reston, VA: National Art Education Association.

Burke, P. (1991). *New perspectives on historical writing*. University Park, PA: The Pennsylvania State University Press.

Cameron, A. (1981). *Daughters of Copper Woman*. Vancouver: Press Gang.

Dreeszen, C. (1994). Local arts agencies: Making a difference in communities. In C. Dreeszen, & P. Korza (Eds.), *Fundamentals of local arts management* (pp. 1-19). Amherst, MA: Arts Extension Service.

Goldbard, A. (1993). Postscript to the past: Notes toward a history of community arts. *High Performance, 16*(4), 23-27.

Lowenthal, D. (1985). *The past is a foreign country*. Cambridge: Cambridge University.

Lummis, C.D. (1996). *Radical democracy*. Ithaca, NY: Cornell, University Press.

Putnam, R.D. (1995). Bowling alone: America's declining social capital. *Journal of Democracy, 6*(1), 65-78.

Shudson, M. (1999). *The good citizen: A history of American civic life*. NY: Free Press.

West, C. (1999). The moral obligations of living in a democratic society. In D. Batstone, & E. Mendieta (Eds.), *The good citizen* (pp. 5-12). NY: Routledge.

Community as Place

The history of community-based art education and community arts is often associated with children, youth, and adults coming together in formal and informal cultural organizations. These places can serve as spaces for public discourse about art and other issues of mutual concern. The following five chapters elaborate on this possibility in relationship to museums, an art school, a university gallery, and a roadside attraction.

This section begins with Barbara Fleisher Zucker's narrative on Anna Curtis Chandler's initiation of art and storytelling programs at the Metropolitan Museum of Art in 1917. Hyungsook Kim continues the focus on museums by describing art education from the 1930s to the 1950s at the Museum of Modern Art in New York City. Both authors discuss art educators and art education at these institutions from a socio-political perspective.

Melody K. Milbrandt's chapter on Lamar and Irene Dodd directs our attention to the relationship of this father and daughter in the context of the development of the School of Fine Arts at the University of Georgia and their careers as artists and art educators. Kathleen Keys and Christine Ballengee Morris continue this attention to art education in higher education through their discussion of the curation and exhibition of cars as art at The Ohio State University—Newark Art Gallery. This exhibit is described as it reflects certain aspects of central Ohio automotive culture.

Automobile travelers' need to stop and stretch their legs has resulted in myriad forms of roadside attractions. Karen M. Kakas's chapter on Ben Hartman's "Historical Rock Garden" concludes this section. New to the discussion of such attractions is Kakas's description of the Rock Garden as a site of community-based arts education.

Doug Blandy
Co-Editor

chapter

1

Anna Curtis Chandler: Art Educator Nonpareil at the Metropolitan Museum of Art

Barbara Fleisher Zucker

Anna Curtis Chandler's 50-year career supports the notion that ideas and techniques popular in one generation are often rediscovered and revived many years later. Furthermore, a review of her varied activities and responsibilities offers information about the formative years of art museum education and the milieu in which she flourished.

Around 1910 a few American art museums began to experiment with storytelling programs. This activity was initiated to reach a wider audience, develop standards of good taste, and to a lesser extent, stifle the growing influence of some popular entertainments such as movies and the Sunday newspaper supplements. By mid-decade several museums, including the Metropolitan Museum of Art (MMA), sponsored story hours, and by the early 1920s their storyteller, Anna Curtis Chandler, was preeminent (Zucker, 1998).

Chandler Begins at MMA

Miss Chandler began her career with the MMA in 1910 as a researcher in the rapidly expanding photographic section of the library.[1] She was 20 years old, a Wellesley College graduate, class of 1909, who majored in art, Latin, and English composition. Chandler remained at Wellesley for a year of graduate study in art and education. Soon after moving to New York City she started taking courses in storytelling and public speaking in area colleges. On weekends she told stories in settlement houses and a hospital for "crippled" children. Many years later Chandler told an interviewer she soon realized that looking up facts, writing descriptive labels, and handling patron requests in the MMA library did not offer her the kind of contact with people she desired (Pennell, 1940).

Aware of the Metropolitan's increasing services to schools and teachers, Chandler expressed her interest in this kind of work to Henry Watson Kent, secretary of the Museum and the person responsible for its educational program. Several months later, in January 1915, the Metropolitan began offering story hours on a limited scale for members' children and groups of children categorized by disability. This development was noted on a graphic summary designed for the Museum's 50th anniversary celebration. In May the Metropolitan hosted the first American conference of art museum instructors. Storytelling was one of the topics discussed (Levy, Vaughan, Forbes, Haney, Elliott, and Scales, 1915). The MMA was also one of the host institutions for story hours sponsored by the School Art League of New York City, an organization formed a few years before to foster the interests of art education in the public schools. Chandler initially presented stories under their auspices and in March 1917 gave a series of three story hours for the children of MMA members. The following month, when the League wanted to employ her as their storyteller for the following year, Kent quickly decided to offer her two story hour series and additional work giving talks in the galleries or telling stories to groups as needed. Although many details were still to be worked out, he emphasized that the Sunday story hours were especially for public school children.

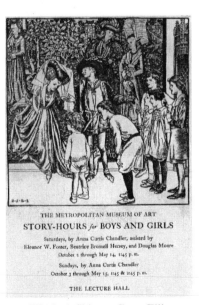

THE METROPOLITAN MUSEUM OF ART
STORY-HOURS *for* BOYS AND GIRLS

Saturdays, by Anna Curtis Chandler, assisted by
Eleanor W. Foster, Beatrice Bromell Hersey, and Douglas Moore
October 2 through May 14, 1:45 p. m.

Sundays, by Anna Curtis Chandler
October 3 through May 15, 1:45 & 2:45 p. m.

THE LECTURE HALL.

Elizabeth Shippen Green Elliot poster, 1926. Art Department, The Free Library of Philadelphia.

In addition to newspaper articles and other announcements, the MMA promoted its first full season of story hours, October 1917 to April 1918, with printed programs

The Saturday and Sunday presentations were the same with one exception. For each, adults were invited to accompany children to hear a story illustrated with stereopticon slides. There was no admission charge. However, only members' children, who attended on Saturday morning, were taken to the galleries to see story-related works of art following the lecture hall program. The Sunday afternoon audience could go to the galleries on their own. In just three months, Chandler drew over 8,700 people to her story hours at the Metropolitan and another 4,000 to nine auditorium talks or stories in schools programs. Most of these activities were illustrated with slides.

Chandler Refines Storytelling and Art Education at the MMA

In the preface to her first book of museum stories *Magic Pictures of the Long Ago* (1918), Chandler said it was the mission of the storyteller to interpret beauty among all peoples of all ages. Therefore, it was appropriate that story hours occur in art museums among beautiful objects. She believed her stories about people and art of different lands would inspire the citizens of tomorrow to have a broad and sympathetic outlook as well as the ability to see worthwhile things. Art museums in Cleveland, Boston, and Worcester invited Chandler to give presentations. Sometimes there was an exchange with their storyteller traveling to the MMA.

Chandler wrote or adapted all of her stories from objects in the museum collection or the lives, times and work of artists and artisans. Her narratives often included factual material embellished with dialogue. The storyteller, she asserted, must make the characters live for the audience. She believed that a sincere interest in people, especially children, was necessary to the success of a story. During her first year, Chandler presented more than 20 different thematic programs. These ranged from ancient Greek to Indian legends. Kent and the Trustees were obviously pleased with her performances and ability to relate to children, school personnel, and members of the museum. Furthermore, her activities mirrored the Metropolitan's educational credo formulated during the spring of 1918 by staff involved in educational work (Howe, 1918). Since Chandler officially transferred from the library to this department the previous fall, she helped shape this statement of principles.

15th Century French costume, Anna Curtis Chandler, ca. 1920s. Hunter College Archives

During the summer of 1918, Kent asked the artist Florence Wyman Ivins to do a poster and programs for Chandler's second season. In October the *New York Times* (Children Getting a Glimpse of Art, 1918) noted that boys and girls from 4 to 15 years of age, of all nationalities and from all sections of the city, were coming for stories and pictures correlated to the treasures in different parts of the museum. Later in the fall, Kent again turned to Ivins, this time to design and sew a costume for Chandler that was worn for the first time the following spring. While the impact of this particular costume is difficult to assess, it must have been substantial, because by the mid 1920s she was known as the "costumed storyteller." Many years later Chandler said she had about 35 costumes representing different countries and periods of history.

Along with her theatrical attire, Chandler did tableau vivants with groups of children, wrote plays, and beginning in 1919 a group of costumed children would present an end-of-the-year performance. To publicize this event, an account with a photograph of a tableau representing an Ivins poster appeared in the MMA *Bulletin* (An Entertainment by the Monitors, 1919). One principal wrote Kent she could not go on vacation without expressing her thanks for the wonderful work the museum was doing to attract children and all that it does to offset lures to evil. Although wishing the work could be extended, the writer realized how difficult it would be to secure other storytellers who would equal Chandler's vivid personality.

In the fall of 1919, in addition to her two weekend story hours series, Chandler met classes at the museum and occasionally traveled to schools. She worked with groups of children after school and became involved with teacher training. In May 1920 Chandler was sent to the annual meeting of the American Association of Museums (AAM) in Washington, DC to give a paper and present a story before a group of area school children and conference participants. In her paper she described the many ways the museum correlated its work with school-work, noting her stories entertained and at the same time instructed. Chandler also touched upon the new plan formulated by the Board of Education and the Metropolitan at the instigation of the director of drawing in the city's elementary schools, Frank H. Collins. This cooperative venture entailed demonstration lessons for teachers who were selected from schools with lanterns [slide projectors] and targeted for students in grades 5 through 9. The model of instruction, always with a class of children from a nearby school, consisted of a talk or story, or sometimes both, followed by relevant slides. Following the demonstration, a synopsis of the lesson, slide list, and sets of slides were given to the art supervisor or teacher. They were expected to reproduce the talk in their school. Her paper and story reached a wider audience when they were published in AAM's *Museum Work* (Chandler, 1920a., 1921). The story was republished in her *Pan the Piper & Other Marvelous Tales* (1923).

In June 1920, a few weeks after the AAM meeting, Chandler and her students were the featured entertainment when the American Federation of Arts (AFA) convened at the Metropolitan. The presentation was a play based on several of her stories as well as a tableau of the Ivins' Sunday story-hour poster. This event, carefully orchestrated by Kent, was designed to call attention to this new method of teaching. At the end of year, Chandler's second of four books of museum stories, *More Magic Pictures of the Long Ago* (1920b.) was published. She also contributed "The Professional Story-Teller" (1920c.) to a book on careers for women.

During the 1920s, Chandler continued her weekend story hours. In mid decade she began giving a Saturday afternoon session for the general public so as to accommodate the number of interested children and adults. This large attendance was driven, in part, by the support of school officials. She also benefited from frequent mention in the city's various newspapers. While some story themes appeared year-after-year, new ones continued to be introduced and familiar ones revised or revitalized. A review of her yearly calendars reflects the development of the Metropolitan's collection and an increased attention to linking presentations to school studies and civic or cultural events. The opening of the American Wing in 1924; the sesquicentennial; and the anniversaries of the birth or death of important artists, historical and literary figures and musicians figured prominently.

In May 1924, in response to a request from the AFA, the Metropolitan sent Chandler to give a talk at the Federation's annual meeting in Washington, DC. Her address "School Children and the Art Museum" was published a few months later (1924). This paper, an overview of the MMA's work with school-age children, also aired some of her concerns regarding resources for teachers and administrative support and suggested a few possible solutions. She called for teachers to be trained in gallery study. Chandler argued that this training should be paid for by the Board of Education as was already being done in a few cities. She also saw the need for a handbook that would help teachers relate school subjects and museum objects, something that she brought to fruition many years later (Chandler, 1943). While she believed the Museum had many ways of reaching children who lived some distance from it, she expressed the hope that some day the MMA and Boards of Education would find a way to provide transportation so all children would have an opportunity to make a few museum visits.

Chandler's Contributions to Teacher Training and Public Education

The success of her story hours and work with teachers led to her increased involvement in various courses offered by the Metropolitan, other area institutions, and eventually to an emerging technology, radio. During the 1925 fall semester she offered "Art Correlation in Connection with Stories from Literature Studied in School Curriculum" for students of the New York Training School. Especially noteworthy was mention in the course description that students would observe two sessions of work with "handicapped" children. This was an audience Chandler met for stories several times a year. During the

1926 spring semester she taught "Story-Telling with Reference to a Greater Enjoyment of Art." This course was open to teachers, students in training, librarians, and others interested in the presentation of subject matter through storytelling and simple plays. In the fall 1926 the Metropolitan announced Chandler would conduct "Picture Study for Elementary and Junior High School Teachers" on Thursdays from October 7 to May 26, 1927. Huger Elliott, director of educational work at the MMA, wrote that the 30-hour course was primarily for teachers but was also open to anyone who cared to enroll. Teachers could receive credit from the Board of Education. Elliott's summary included a brief description of the course plan and named the invited speakers. The *New York Sun* ("Picture Study" for Teachers, 1926) published the week-by-week schedule. This newspaper also noted that this new course was specifically designed to train teachers to meet the requirements of the syllabus in picture study, something relatively new in the city's elementary schools.

Coinciding with the course announcement was the release of a story-hour poster created by the artist Elizabeth Shippen Green Elliott. This image also appeared on the front cover of the September 1926 MMA *Bulletin* and was published in a lengthy newspaper article (East Side, West Side, 1926). See page 2 for illustration. The image of figures stepping out of a tapestry appears to have been inspired by a work in MMA's collection. Chandler wore a similar costume in connection with stories bringing paintings, sculptures, and tapestries to life.

From 1926 through 1933, Chandler continued to offer courses at the Metropolitan that were designed for teachers and interested others. In the fall of 1927, in addition to teaching an afternoon course for the MMA, she offered an evening course "The Humanizing of Art through Stories, Illustrated Talks, and Simple Plays" for Hunter College. The *New York Sun* reported that (Story Telling Course, 1927) it was "for those interested in art and in the art of story telling with reference to a greater enjoyment of art, and for those who wish to relate art to the school curriculum, humanizing the one and vitalizing the other." This course for Hunter lead to another evening class the following fall that met at both the College and the Museum. In her 1929-1930 course for the MMA "Daily Life as Told in Art" she stressed the development of costume, including study of costuming a play. This emphasis was designed to attract teachers of the domestic arts and dramatics. Echoing her earlier article in a New York newspaper, Geraldine Runchey (1930) noted that Chandler's new method of dramatizing art had been criticized by some who were not attuned to it. However, she also noted that Chandler's methods were not only in line with progressive educational theory, but also with the new practices art museums were using to present their gallery objects. The Metropolitan Museum of Art, Runchey concluded, was making itself a great center and union of all arts and Chandler's successful work was a part of this effort.

In 1929 Chandler published two more books, her fourth book of museum stories and the first of collective biographies (*A Voyage to Treasure Land, Story-Lives of Master Artists*, 1929b., 1929a.). This same year two of her earlier titles appeared on a selected list, "A Ready Reference Library," (1929) prepared by a committee of the influential North Central Association and reprinted in *School Arts Magazine*.

Another activity not specifically part of Chandler's responsibilities at the Metropolitan, but related to them, was serving on the New York Story League board of directors from 1929 to 1934. She also contributed a chapter ("The Story in Art Teaching," 1934) to the League's book, *The Story-Telling Hour*, describing the pioneering work of story specialists working with different audiences.

In 1932, Chandler discovered a new venue for dramatic storytelling when she did two nationally broadcast programs for the Columbia Broadcasting System's *American School of the Air*. These programs were "'Portrait of George Washington' by Gilbert Stuart" and "'A Northeaster' by Winslow Homer." She replaced Henry Turner Bailey who died the previous year (Keith & Johnson, 1931). The success of these two programs (Keith, 1932) lead to her 13-program series "Treasure Trails in Art" in 1935-1936 (Johnson, 1935). Some of these programs included dramatizations with many of the parts acted by children from the New York Professional Children's School (Pennell, 1940). Chandler also prepared the curriculum guide for these programs. A few months after the series ended there was an exhibit of artwork from children around the country who listened to her broadcasts (Exhibit of the 'School of the Air', 1936).

Chandler Leaves MMA

The economic situation of the early 1930s, and administrative changes at the Metropolitan, led to a reassessment of its programs and responsibilities. Coffin, the MMA's new president, signaled a shift in emphasis from art appreciation for elementary school-age children to teaching history to high school students (Coffin, 1933). Emphasis was no longer placed on art from the Metropolitan's exhibits. Coffin noted that because of the large number of pupils in the public schools, it was impossible for the Museum to attempt to educate all of them within the walls of the Metropolitan. This change, combined with some existing dissatisfaction with Chandler's story hour program, led to her resignation. During her last full year at the Metropolitan she drew 80,000 to her story hours. Without Chandler the Museum's program faded. Later Winifred E. Howe (1946) wrote, "Until her resignation in 1934 she was the Museum storyteller, and many young people in New York laid the foundation for an appreciation of art in her story hours" (p. 167).

Even after Chandler was no longer officially connected with the Metropolitan, she capitalized on her long affiliation with it. In the fall of 1934 she began a series of free Sunday afternoon programs for children and interested adults at the 92nd Street Y's Kaufmann Auditorium. She was billed as the costumed storyteller and author. These presentations, supported by the Board of Education and a number of community organizations, followed the same format as those given previously at the Museum. Chandler described these illustrated programs as both educational and entertaining. They were planned to correlate with art, literature, music, and science and lead to a closer acquaintance with New York's museums and places of historical and civic interest. Chandler proposed that children and interested adults would form good habits for the use of leisure time as a result of their attendance.

Chandler offered these Kaufmann Auditorium programs until the end of 1936 when, again due to economic pressures, institutional change, and her own professional agenda, they ceased. During this period, in addition to her Sunday presentations and radio broadcasts, Chandler started teaching at Hunter College, wrote a series of articles on picture study for *Grade Teacher* (1935-1937), and published more books and articles for young readers. Chandler received her masters degree in 1940 from New York University. Three years later she was awarded an EdD from the same institution. In 1941 she was appointed head of the Audio-Visual Enrichment Program at the Hunter College Elementary. This was a school for gifted children. She held this position until her retirement in 1960. Chandler died in 1969 at age 79.

Endnotes

[1]Unless otherwise noted facts and statements associated with the life and work of Anna Curtis Chandler were derived from correspondence and other materials held by The Metropolitan Museum of Art, Wellesley College, The 92nd Street Y, The New York Public Library, The Archives of American Art, and Hunter College. The author is indebted to these archives and libraries for access to their collections.

References

Chandler, A.C. (1918). *Magic pictures of the long ago.* NY: Henry Holt.

Chandler, A.C. (1920a). Children's work at the Metropolitan Museum of Art. *Museum Work, 3* (3), 85-89.

Chandler, A.C. (1920b). *More magic pictures of the long ago.* NY: Henry Holt.

Chandler, A.C. (1920c). The professional storyteller. In C. Filene (Ed.). *Careers for women* (pp. 116-118). Boston, MA: Houghton Mifflin. (1934). (Rev. ed.) pp. 398-400.

Chandler, A.C. 1921). The spirit of the Persian rug tells of the mighty hero, Rustem. *Museum Work, 3* (4), frontispiece, 110-117.

Chandler, A.C. (1923). *Pan the piper & other marvelous tales.* New York: Harper and Brothers.

Chandler, A.C. (1924). School children and the art museum. *The American Magazine of Art, 15* (10), 508-513.

Chandler, A.C. (1929a). *Story-lives of master artists.* NY: Frederick A. Stokes.

Chandler, A.C. (1929b). *A voyage to treasure land.* NY: Harper and Brothers.

Chandler, A.C. (1934). The story in art teaching. In C. S. Bailey (Ed.), *The story-telling hour* (pp. 159-179). NY: Dodd, Mead.

Chandler, A.C. (1935-1937). Picture study. *Grade Teacher, 53* (1)-54 (10).

Chandler, A.C. (1943). *Audio-Visual Enrichment of Art, Language Arts, and the Social Studies—A Handbook for Teachers of the Junior High Schools and for Teachers-in-Training in New York City and the Metropolitan Area.* Unpublished doctoral dissertation, New York University, NY.

Children getting a glimpse of art. (1918, October 13). *The New York Times*, s. 8, p. 2.

Coffin. W.S. (1933). The role of the Metropolitan Museum of Art in the educational system of New York City. *Bulletin of the Metropolitan Museum of Art, 28* (9), 150-152.

East side, west side, children from all around the town invited to story hours at museum. (1926, September 22). *The New York Sun,* no page.

An entertainment by the monitors. (1919). *Bulletin of the Metropolitan Museum of Art, 14* (7), 165.

Exhibit of the "School of the Air" of the Columbia Broadcasting Company System. (1936, June 13). *School and Society, 43,* 810.

Howe, W.E. (1918). The museum's educational credo. *Bulletin of the Metropolitan Museum of Art, 13* (9), 192-193.

Howe, W.E. (1946). *A history of the Metropolitan Museum of Art, 1905-1941* (Vol. 2). NY: Columbia University, p. 167.

Johnson, H. (Comp.). (1935). *The American School of the Air teachers manual and classroom guide, 1935-1936.* NY: Columbia Broadcasting System. pp. 6-7, 10-11, 28-33.

Keith, A. (1932). Museum cooperation with educational broadcasting. *Museum News, 10* (11), 8.

Keith, A. & Johnson, H. (1931). (Comps.). *The American School of the Air teachers manual and classroom guide, 1931-1932.* NY: Columbia Broadcasting System. pp. 3, 6-7, 9, 32-33, 35-36.

Levy, F., Vaughan, A., Forbes, R., Haney, J., Elliott, H., & Scales, L. (1915). Methods of using art museums. *American Art Annual, 12,* pp. 15-16, 21-22, 25-30.

Pennell, P. (1940, July 28). Energetic daughter of Maine is author of children's books. *Portland Telegraph-Press Herald,* no page.

"Picture study" for teachers: Metropolitan Museum course will train in instruction of art appreciation. (1926, September 17). *The New York Sun,* no page.

A ready reference library. (1929). *The School Arts Magazine, 28* (6), p. 9.

Runchey, G. (1930). Art appreciation for children: the work of Anna Curtis Chandler in the Metropolitan Museum of Art, New York. *School Arts Magazine, 29* (5), 316-320, ix.

Story-telling course. (1927, September 14*). The New York Sun,* no page.

Zucker, B. (1998). Competition for audience: museum storytellers and "the movies" (1910-1920). *Animation Journal, 7* (1), 35-51.

Art Education in the Museum of Modern Art (1930s-1950s)

Hyungsook Kim

The Regent Charter of the Museum of Modern Art (MoMA), drawn up in 1929, states that the MoMA was established and maintained for the purpose of "encouraging and developing the study of modern arts and the appreciation of such arts to manufacture and practical life, and furnishing popular instruction" (Hunter, 1984, p. 9). This Charter indicates that the MoMA was founded for the dual purposes of "popular instruction" in modern art as well as "productive scholarship" on modern art. This charter responded to the belief that the public did not fully understand and appreciate modern art.

Written histories of the MoMA have typically focused on collectors, collections, and exhibitions (Goodyear, 1943; Hunter, 1984; Lynes, 1973). Histories regarding educational efforts at the MoMA have been ignored or considered a "marginal" area of study by art educators and museum professionals.

This chapter rediscovers unknown and ignored shifts and changes in the educational practices and mission of the MoMA from the 1930s to the 1950s. My examination of the historical documents of the MoMA shows that there were shifts in the development of art education. These shifts were influenced by external social and cultural changes of the time. In this chapter I will discuss phenomena arising during four moments in the history of the MoMA: (a) phases associated with the founding of the Museum (1929-1934); (b) shifts in the educational mission (1935-1938); (c) the practice of Progressive Education at the MoMA with emphasis on Victor D'Amico's approach to art education at the Museum (1939-1950s); and (d) the emergence of a new approach to art education during the mid-1950s.

Establishing Education at the Museum of Modern Art

In 1929, the Board of Regents of the University of the State of New York, acting on behalf of the State Education Department, granted a provisional charter for:

> establishing and maintaining in the City of New York, a museum of modern art, encouraging and developing the study of modern arts and the application of such arts to manufacture and practical life, and furnishing popular instruction (Hunter, 1984, p. 9).

The Regent Charter of the MoMA indicates that the Museum was founded provisionally to determine whether or not there existed a sufficient public interest in modern art in order to justify the establishment of a permanent institution devoted to the collection, exhibition, and study of works of the modern school.

Clearly, the MoMA charter stressed "dual purposes" in the mission. First, to encourage and develop the study of modern arts. To fulfill this mission, the MoMA attempted to enhance and define the value of modern art through research. Second, to educate the public through "popular instruction" of modern art. The Museum, as a public-relations organization, used its artistic resources to "educate" and elevate public taste through a tempered messianic spirit.

The dual nature of the purpose of the MoMA was the central idea supporting the development of the Museum. *The Annual Report of 1933-34 (Director's Partial Report)* describes these dual purposes as: (a) production and (b) distribution (The Museum of Modern Art, 1934). Maintaining the permanent collection is definitely a production function of the Museum, whereas changing exhibitions and presenting them to the public is distribution. Although the dual purposes of production and distribution are stressed, the *Annual Report* of the Museum indicates that the ultimate purpose of the MoMA was production:

A proper balance between production and distribution can be obtained in the Museum only by emphasis on the former. More time and planning and money must be given to production. It cannot be carried on in the atmosphere of a newspaper office (The Museum of Modern Art, 1934, p. 3).

Moreover, the notion of distribution seems to be limited to exhibition rather than various possible potential educational programs and activities. In other words, during the period form 1929 to 1933, the MoMA did not see educational activities and programs as a part of distribution. The aim of the Museum was to bring about widespread understanding and appreciation of modern art by exhibiting living artists' works.

A Shift in the Educational Mission

The meaning of education is socially constructed and conditioned by historical, social, and cultural phenomena. These factors not only affect schools, but any institution that has an educational mission as part of its charter. Consequently, the educational value of exhibitions at the MoMA underwent a shift around 1935 because of a shift in historical and social conditions in the United States. One critical external factor, the Great Economic Depression, surely had an effect on the educational mission of the MoMA.

One important shift of external contexts in American society around 1935 was President Franklin D. Roosevelt's New Deal Relief Program. In March 1933 President Roosevelt articulated the keynote of his administration's policy to deal with unemployment. As one aspect of the policy, the Government became a patron of the arts, the President asserting that "the provision of work for those people at occupations which will conserve their skills is of prime importance" (Rawlins, 1981, p. 131).

Artists who had always belonged to a marginal occupation received a particularly devastating blow with the Depression. Roosevelt's programs were the first time, in the history of the United States, that the Federal government officially supported the arts. The New Deal Relief Programs for artists were a marked departure from the American tradition of private philanthropy (Rawlins, 1981, p. 137). In order to survive the worst years of the Depression, most museums stepped up their educational efforts by employing artists. Financial necessity settled the old debate among museum professionals regarding whether the central role of art institutions should be conservational or educational. The MoMA was not an exception.

At the height of the New Deal Relief Programs, the MoMA attempted to find a way to contribute to its role as educational institution. During this time, Artemas Packard was employed to find out how the MoMA could most effectively aid in the development of esthetic values in American life (Packard, 1935-36). Packard assumed that the trustees intended to set up an Education Department in the near future and thought that it would be worthwhile to examine the nature of the problems of building up relations with schools and colleges. He made some suggestions to the trustees as to what the position of the MoMA should be in relation to other museums and to schools and colleges. He saw the role of the MoMA as assisting "the universities in working out a program of art study which will be more consistent with the needs of the student and less unfavorable to a sympathetic interest in contemporary art" (Packard, 1938, p. 22). Additionally, Packard seriously urged effective collaboration between the schools and the MoMA. For instance, he proposed that the Museum could set an example of methods of instruction in devising special exhibitions and docent services for groups of children from the schools. Packard's recommendations on the educational role of the MoMA gave some direction to the Advisory Committee on the best way to integrate art with other subjects in the curriculum. In 1937, the Department of Education was established at the MoMA. Packard saw this department as one way of achieving popular instruction.

> Theoretically, inasmuch as the Museum of Modern Art is an educational institution, its various departments may be thought of as each devoted to some specific educational enterprise. In fact, however, very little attention is given, within the present organization, to a consideration of the educational value of any of the Museum's activities. The Trustees have hoped this report might assist them in planning of an Education Department whose function would be to supervise various types of instructional services such as are now commonly expected of a public art museum. There can be no doubt

as to the great need within the organization for some agency which can devote all its attention to the business of coordinating the expanding educational activities of the various departments, of seeking to secure consistency of effort with reference to the main purposes of the institution in planning new activities, and of keeping in touch with other educational institution (Packard, 1935-36, p. 17).

Packard maintained that the MoMA should awaken public interest in all forms of modern art. For popularizing modern art, the progressive education theory, which had become the basis for the educational models in schools by the late 1930s, was adopted. Yet, Packard maintained that the MoMA should be aware of the paradoxical implications of establishing a program of education that was to be independent of, but equal to the museum's curatorial activities. If not, according to Packard, the MoMA might fall into "the error of encouraging the one to the detriment of the other and impede the development of a broader understanding which may harmonize their apparent contradictions" (Packard, 1938, p. 64).

The Department of Education at the MoMA had a threefold purpose: First to help meet the needs of children and adults seeking to understand art for their personal satisfaction; second, to promote among the general public an understanding of the value of creative art experience in everyday life; and third, to stimulate the teaching profession in promoting art for the purpose of general education (The Museum of Modern Art, 1960). The program of the Education Department initially consisted of teaching 4 high school classes a week, preparing and circulating visual material to 10 high schools, and operating the Young People's Gallery (The Museum of Modern Art, 1946, p. 14).

Progressive Education, Modern Art, and the Museum of Modern Art

The concern for popular instruction was not fully realized until 10 years after the opening of the MoMA. As we have already seen, the purposes of the Museum, under the guidance of the first director, Alfred Barr, were to invent a history of modern art and make modern art a part of the discipline of art history. As the economic depression heightened during the mid 1930s, the MoMA began to pay more attention to its educational mission for the general public. Yet, it was 10 years after the opening of the MoMA that dramatic changes in the implementation of its mission of education for the public occurred. A number of literary works published in 1939 discuss and emphasize the educational role of the MoMA. For instance, Sachs (1939) indicates that American museums continued to be not only exhibition centers and repositories of treasures, as in Europe, but also educational centers. *The Annual Report* of the Museum of Modern Art describes this particular year, 1939, as a period of "remarkable growth and achievement" in terms of the Museum's educational mission for the public (The Museum of Modern Art, 1940, p. 9).

The year 1939 marked a new beginning for the MoMA. The Museum entered its permanent building and as a consequence increased space for exhibitions and educational programs. Nelson A. Rockefeller was elected to succeed A. Conger Goodyear as president of the MoMA. In addition to internal shifts at the MoMA, external factors, such as the new movement in general educational reform contributed to the construction of a new meaning of education at the Museum.

By the late 1930s, the ideals of Progressive Education had become the basis for the educational reform prevalent in private schools, as well as in public schools in upper middle-class suburbs (Morgan, 1995, p. 154). Because Packard's report based on progressive education philosophy was taken seriously at the MoMA, Victor D'Amico was hired by Barr to design and implement educational programs. D'Amico played a pivotal role in the history of museum education after the MoMA entered its permanent building.

Relying upon the theories of John Dewey regarding people and art, D'Amico developed and elaborated educational programs and activities at the MoMA for children between the ages of 3 and 18, veterans, and a large class of adults. D'Amico also founded the Museum's Young People's Gallery, the War Veterans Art Center, and the People's Art Center.

D'Amico's programs for the MoMA won national as well as international acclaim. His programs were funded through grants from the Whitney Foundation, Carnegie Corporation, Rockefeller Foundation, and the General Education Board (The Museum of Modern Art, 1940, p. 23).

Art Education at the Museum of Modern Art during the Mid Century

In the mid 1950s, the philosophy of art education at the MoMA shifted. The theory of Progressive Education was questioned and challenged by the Department of Education of the Museum. During this time, there was a struggle between opposing forces in the Education Department. Opposition occurred because of changes in the external contexts of the time.

In the mid-1950s, a quarter-century after the founding of the MoMA, the art movement of the day, the ideals of educational reform, and the American sociopolitical circumstances shifted rapidly. The Soviet Union broke America's nuclear monopoly with the explosion of an atom bomb. Nationalist fervor reached epidemic proportions after the Russian space launch in 1957 (Morgan, 1995, p.161). Under the competitive pressures of this period, the ideal of Progressive education lost its influence, and the U. S. Office of Education administered art education, with the purpose of the development of new knowledge for solving educational problems. A curriculum reform movement was initiated to sponsor the curriculum projects in science and mathematics (Efland, 1990, p. 237). In the art world, Abstract Expressionism, which had epitomized the power of action and experience, gave way to much more intellectual and emotionally cooler art movements, such as Pop Art, Minimalism, and Conceptualism (Morgan, 1995, p. 163).

Corresponding to these social and cultural shifts, the MoMA initiated changes in its museum education. Creative art education was challenged and questioned. There was also a shift away from the ideals of Progressive Education among the members of the Committee on Art Education (COAE).[1]

From its inception, the COAE defended the ideal of progressive education, and, during the 1950s, practitioners of creative art education in the COAE came to be associated with the MoMA. The Museum strongly supported the new organization, because of the link between modern art and Progressive Education, as well as D'Amico's commitment to its programs and organization.

COAE was formed to defend creative art education in the face of economic and national interests that increasingly dominated the national education agenda. The purpose of COAE was to "bring together educators interested in formulating a basic philosophy of art education and promoting creative teaching on the highest possible level" (The Museum of Modern Art, 1951, p. 17). However, by the mid-1950s, theoretical differences among the members of the Committee began to emerge. D'Amico's focus on aesthetic matters was not shared by all. Other members proposed a new teaching method, the art historical approach to museum education. That corresponded to the shift of educational atmosphere of that time:

> The guardians of self-expression attempted to meet the crisis [of the paradigm shift in education] by arguing that it could foster creativity in children which would enable them to become creative adults in fields like science and mathematics...an argument which never convinced anyone (Efland, 1992, p. 2).

By the mid 1950s the ideal of Progressive Education at the Museum was dead. D'Amico's experimental programs emphasizing that 'making art' was the most significant learning process for the appreciation of art seemed increasingly out of step with the art historical approach to museum education.

Conclusion

Even though popular instruction was mentioned in the Regent Charter of the MoMA, education was not fully considered during the founding period of the Museum. Few primary sources record the Museum's efforts to fulfill the educational mission for the public. These sources tell us only that the educational mission seems to have been marginalized compared to activities associated with collecting and exhibition works of modern art. Yet, with the Great Depression, in order to survive, the Museum stepped up its educational efforts in order to obtain outside funding. This effort helped redefine the Museum as an educational institution.

During the 1930s through the 1950s, Progressive Education theory became the prevalent educational philosophy at the MoMA. This trend in museum education at the MoMA shifted during the mid 1950s as a new educational paradigm sought to provide models of the "disciplines and show how they could be used in curriculum reform" (Morgan, 1995, p. 168).

Endnotes

[1]The Committee on Art Education (COAE, at first called the Committee on Art in American Education and Society) was founded in January, 1943 by D'Amico to promote his educational ideals of progressive education.

References

Efland, A. (1992). History of art education as criticism: On the use of the past. In Amburgy, P. & Soucy, D. (Eds.). *The history of art education: Proceedings from the second Penn State Conference, 1989* (pp. 1-11). Reston, VA: The National Art Education Association.

Goodyear, C. (1943). *The Museum of Modern Art: The first ten years.* New York: The Museum of Modern Art.

Hunter, S. (1984). Introduction. In The Museum of Modern Art (Ed.), *The Museum of Modern Art, New York: The history and the collection* (pp. 7-40). New York: Harry N. Abrams, Inc.

Lynes, R. (1973). *Good old modern: An intimate portrait of the Museum of Modern Art.* New York: Atheneum.

Morgan, C. (1995). From modernist utopia to cold war reality: A critical moment in museum education. In The Museum of Modern Art (Ed). *The Museum of Modern Art at mid-century: Continuity and change* (pp. 151-173). New York: The Museum of Modern Art.

The Museum of Modern Art. (1934). *Annual report, 1933-34: Director's partial report.* The Museum of Modern Art Archives: Box 1/1.

The Museum of Modern Art. (1940). *Annual report to the board of trustees and the corporation members of the Museum of Modern Art, June 30, 1939 – July 1, 1940.* New York: The Museum of Modern Art.

The Museum of Modern Art. (1946, February). *The Museum of Modern Art Bulletin, 1944-1945* (Vol. XIII, No. 3). New York: The Museum of Modern Art.

The Museum of Modern Art. (1951). *The Museum of Modern Art Bulletin, 1951.* New York: The Museum of Modern Art.

The Museum of Modern Art. (1960, May). *The art in art education: 18th annual conference of the national committee on art education.* The

Museum of Modern Art Archives: The History of the Education Department, Box 1/1.

Packard, A. (1935-36). *Report on the Museum of Modern Art: Part two the function of the museum in general education.* The Museum of Modern Art Archives: Reports and Pamphlets, Box 3/14.

Packard, A. (1938*). A report on the development of the Museum of Modern Art: Based on a survey of the present organization and activities of the Museum conducted during the years 1935-36.* The Museum of Modern Art Archives: Reports and Pamphlets, Box 3/14.

Rawlins, K. E. (1981). *The educational metamorphosis of the American art museum.* Unpublished doctoral dissertation, Stanford University.

Sachs, P. J. (1939, Sep.). Why is a museum of art? *Architectural Forum.* Chicago, IL. Archives of American Art, Smithsonian Institution, SI-1787 (4-71), Roll No. 5092.

chapter

3

Lamar and Irene Dodd: Father and Daughter Influencing the Development of the Visual Arts in Georgia

Melody K. Milbrandt

Although I had causally known Irene Dodd for almost a decade it wasn't until she exhibited a retrospective of her work at the Lowndes-Valdosta Cultural Arts Center in January of 1997 that I began to understand what a remarkable legacy she provides the state of Georgia. The daughter of Lamar Dodd, the first department head at the University of Georgia Department of Art, Irene spoke of her father's influence on her career as an artist and art teacher. As she spoke she produced several journal/sketchbooks created between the ages of 11 and 12 (Dodd, 1953-54; Dodd, 1954). The pen-and-ink drawings and written descriptions of her travels through Europe with her family in the early 1950s were amazing. Scenes of gondola boats, St. Mark's Cathedral, Roman aqueducts, and the Arles countryside punctuated the pages of written description. She pointed out that the themes begun in her childhood sketchbooks had continued throughout her life as an artist. Looking around the gallery I saw masterful watercolors of St. Mark's Cathedral and Venetian waterways, as well as scenes from some of her favorite locations on Monhegan Island, Maine.

Upon closer examination, I found the sketchbooks contained not only remarkable un-childlike renderings, but also impressive descriptions of art and architecture (Dodd, 1953-54; Dodd, 1954). Irene described

Irene Dodd, Sketchbook/Journal, cathedral at Tours, France, exterior and interior,
February 12, 1954, age 12.

paying eight cents to enter the Prado Museum in Madrid, enjoying the
El Greco room and then running to the Van Weyden room where she
was impressed with a large painting called "The Descent." She wrote
in her journal (Dodd, 1953-1954),

> In this I noticed a very brownish gold underpainting and the strokes
> were vertical. The red color in the eyes is nice on the crying women
> among the green flowers. Most men were wearing cloppers and
> long red stockings, including the man holding Christ with Leonardo
> da Vinci beard. As I left the painting I noticed that the sides were
> painted like a frame. (February 7, 1954, p. 270)

In her journal (Dodd, 1953-54), Irene recalled enjoying the flat color
and pattern of early Renaissance painting. Her notes confess to
wandering away from her parents to investigate a cathedral painting.
She also accompanied her father to the studio of de Chirico, but was
not impressed by the work of the Moderns. Amid the sophisticated
description of the artwork and countryside there are periodic notes that
reveal Irene, the young adolescent, and her close relationship with her
father (Dodd, 1953-1954):

Lunch, and then Daddy and I walked five blocks to the Giotto
mural. It was still snowing. The streets had snow and then a thin
layer of ice underneath. It was treacherous footing and Daddy and I
held on to each other. Rounding a corner we got hit in the face with
snow, snow, snow. We managed to find the sidewalk and get up off
of the street. Man, it was really coming down now. (January 26,
1954, p. 152)

After hearing Irene's presentation I realized how little I knew about
Irene's career and her father's role in the development of art programs
in my adopted state of Georgia. Irene agreed to meet with me and
discuss her father, Lamar Dodd, and his commitment to art and art
education not only at the University of Georgia, but across the region.
As we sat in her home in Valdosta, Georgia in the spring of 1998, Irene
was recovering from hip surgery. However, her blue eyes maintained
their characteristic determination and directness as she spoke. She
recalled her formative experiences growing up on the University of
Georgia campus in the early 1950s. She also shared her memories of
her father as well as other influential artists and art teachers from that
period, who influenced her teaching philosophy and practice.

Lamar Dodd, Artist and Art Administrator

Lamar Dodd was born in Fairburn, Georgia on September 22, 1909 to
Reverend and Mrs. Francis Jefferson Dodd, the 3rd son of 5 children.
Shortly after his birth the family moved to a large Greek revival home,
The Oaks, in LaGrange (Arthur, 1996). By the age of 12, Lamar's
drawing and painting abilities had been discovered and encouraged by
his sixth grade teacher and his parents. Hoping their son would
become an architect, the Dodds helped Lamar arrange for art lessons at
the LaGrange Female College (his mother's alma mater), in exchange
for mowing the grass, hauling ashes and other odd jobs as payment for
the lessons. Undaunted at being at a girl's school, Dodd became
something of the class mascot, sitting among the young women
classmates, absorbed in his drawing assignments.

In the South, in the early 20th century, advanced study in the arts was
impossible. Lamar, pressured by his family to become an architect,
attended Georgia Institute for Technology in 1926. This was the

bleakest period of Dodd's life. He had a nervous breakdown and became so ill he returned home to LaGrange. He regained his strength and began painting again. He also took a job teaching art in a nearby small town. By 1928 Dodd knew he would have to leave the South to further develop his artistic vision (Eiland, 1996).

From Georgia, the trip to New York was 30 hours by train. Lamar chose to attend The Art Students League, in part, because it was a nonstructured program that allowed students to choose their own teachers. Dodd enrolled in a drawing course with George Bridgeman and a painting studio with George Luks. Later instructors included Boardman Robinson and Richard Lahey, John Steuart Curry, and Jean Charlot. Admittedly influenced by the Ashcan School, Dodd adopted the palette and even some of the compositional devices of John Sloan, Reginald Marsh, and Charles Scheeler (Arthur, 1996). The South was his region, and it became his central subject. Dodd became a leading painter among Deep South artists and writers whose three consistent themes were race, religion, and the land. According to Eiland (1996), Dodd emphasized the "distinct character of the place and he invested his subjects with attributes that particularized them, made them specific, even realistic as landmarks, but also somehow universal." (p. 25) Critical artistic success came relatively soon. The Philadelphia Annual Watercolor Exhibition accepted a watercolor by Dodd in the fall of 1929. In 1930 Dodd returned to Georgia to marry his high school sweetheart, Mary Lehmann, and to paint his region for a year. During this sabbatical from New York he held a one-man show at the High Museum in Atlanta and won a purchase award from the Southern States Art League. He returned to New York in 1931 for 3 more years of study and shows. Other one-man shows and exhibits in New York led to numerous purchases, including one by the Metropolitan Museum. Admirers concluded that the 23 year old painter was representative a new spirit of art in the South (Eiland, 1996).

Lamar and Mary did not escape the economic hardships of the Depression. In 1933 when offered a position in an art supply store in Birmingham, Alabama, Dodd moved back to his Southern homeland. He continued to paint in his home studio and by 1934 his reputation as a successful regionalist painter was firmly established. From 1929 to 1949 Dodd's resume is filled with important exhibits, awards, and purchases from across the nation (Eiland, 1996).

In 1937, due to his growing regional and national reputation, the University of Georgia invited Lamar Dodd to Athens as an artist-in-residence. One year later at the age of 27, he was appointed head of the art department. When Dodd arrived at Georgia there was no organized art department. Three teachers were scattered throughout several university departments; one in agriculture with the extension service, one with home economics, and one in the School of Fine Arts. Dodd saw this as an indication of the low status the arts held in the South. The next year he moved all teachers into one school with himself as head in 1939. The first year his new School of Fine Arts attracted nine majors and was housed in the basement of a residential building. During his 38-year tenure, Dodd guided the University of Georgia Art Department to one of the largest in the nation, with more than 700 majors and a faculty of 53. Some of the art educators hired by Dodd were Sibl Brown, Frank Wachoviak, Edmund Feldman, W. Robert Nix, and Robert Clements. Today the slide library boasts a collection of over 25,000 objects, and a complex of campus buildings house a variety of diverse art department areas (Eiland, 1996; McCutheon and Nix, 1987).

Lamar Dodd saw the artist as much a part of the community as the banker or plumber. In an un-Bohemian way he initiated an art movement in the South that was recognized throughout the nation (Lamar Dodd: In an unbohemian way, 1949). He organized auctions, exhibitions, and artist lectures that raised awareness of the new art department and provided forums for artists to interact with the community. Dodd continued his artwork almost until the end of this life in 1996. In later years he became primarily recognized for his administrative achievements at the University of Georgia. While never earning a college degree, Dodd received several honorary doctoral degrees and served on countless regional and national boards for art and art education. In 1982 LaGrange College named its new visual arts building after Dodd and in 1995 the Board of Regents named the University of Georgia art department established by Dodd, the Lamar Dodd School of Art (Eiland, 1996).

Lamar Dodd as Teacher and Parent

Irene and I discussed her father's influence on her artistic and philosophical development. Irene (personal communication, 1998) recalled that in her youth,

> Art itself was never pushed upon me. I think I was encouraged to
> develop all of my abilities, but art was always there. As a child I
> remember making art in my father's studio whenever I chose. I
> often lay sprawled on the rug on the floor with paint or crayons. I
> have paintings done there between the ages of 2 to 4, using large
> arm movements to draw with a brush. I often accompanied my
> father on painting trips to Monhegan Island, off the coast of Maine.
> I had a sketchbook and drew from age eight. It's been most interest-
> ing to me that many of the Monhegan themes, and others introduced
> in my childhood have remained with me throughout my life. I don't
> remember attending very structured art classes as a child. I did
> attend some local informal classes in Athens where we had a
> storytime then painted our impressions of the story. Father and
> others advocated for art in the public schools at both the elementary
> and high school level. We did get a high school art program during
> the 1950s and of course, today the public schools now have art
> education programs. My father saw his art as an outgrowth of the
> people around him. He saw integral connections between art and
> life and wanted to make art more accessible to others. I'm sure he
> made a conscious decision to return to the South to teach and to
> connect the art department to civic life as his larger work of art.
> Those were not values popular in the avant garde art world of New
> York in the 1930s-40s so I guess by those standards he was very
> traditional. Southern visual artists seemed to have a harder time
> finding a forum for their work, so I think he saw his role in Georgia
> as providing a way to open the state to the larger art work in a
> palatable manner. He was determined to offer opportunities for
> young artists here to connect to the larger art world outside of this
> region.

In 1953-54, when Irene was in the 7th grade, she accompanied her
parents on an extended trip to Europe. It was a very unusual 10-month
trip, primarily designed for Lamar to visit museums and galleries and
to develop resources and contacts for the university (Arthur, 1996).
Irene was allowed to make up schoolwork prior to the trip, since it was
definitely an educational venture. Irene recalls she read a lot of art
history prior to visits to museums. She felt confident that she was
prepared and often informed the adults on the trip about the historical

Irene Dodd, "Scenes of Italy," pen and ink, 1954, age 12.

context of the art. Her love of art history continued throughout her life. Irene's journal-sketchbooks describe the places visited, but often she felt she could better describe something if she drew it. She frequently drew at the site and then upon returning to the hotel at the end of the day she wrote about the experience. Sometimes while writing in the evening she added a drawing based on a postcard of the place (personal communication, March 7, 1998).

Irene readily admits she had an extraordinary childhood. Her opportunities for travel and interaction with the art world were numerous. However, art was never forced upon Irene and she avoided pursuing a career in art for many years. As a child Lamar encouraged his daughter to trust her intuition and look at the world around her. Because he saw she had some ability in art he kept art materials available for her, but he was wise in not forcing art instruction upon her. Irene unconsciously moved away from the visual arts and her father understood her need to develop in other areas. His primary goal was that she develop as many of her abilities as possible (personal communication, March 7, 1998). Irene enjoyed music and had a good voice, so she stopped seriously creating art at about age 12 and initially majored in music and psychology at Duke University. She later returned to college to earn an MFA in the visual arts at the University of Georgia. She (personal communication, March 7, 1998) recounts her early experience as an artist,

> I think had I been a man I might have had more of a springboard into art, than (I did) as a woman....At that time I think women were obviously still struggling to break into major galleries. I had avoided becoming an artist I think because I did not want to be seen as only "Lamar Dodd's daughter" yet, once I decided to do it, the shadow (of my father) though large, wasn't large enough to deter me. I don't think having a well-known father was a professional advantage, given the role of women at that time...There may have been a certain amount of curiosity initially about Lamar Dodd's daughter, so "who I was" might have been initially helpful, but after that point you have to prove yourself through your work and I think that's the way it should be. Of course, had my father stayed in New York my career might have been different there too, but I spent time in New York as a graduate student and I knew it wasn't me. When you enter a field you have to be aware of the field you're playing in, and understand how it functions. Whether you're male or female, where you live, its all a part of the field you enter. You have to decide if you're going to play or not. You have to be at peace with yourself about what you do. But you have to decide if you're willing to play the game your field demands. I chose not to play that game in New York, because it wasn't me. Sometimes you have to go and experience something like that for a while to figure that out.

Other Educational Influences

When Lamar Dodd arrived at the university he brought "new life" to art and art education in Georgia through teachers, and the artists he employed. Irene (personal communication, March 7, 1998) remembers seeing Ames and Garrard's "Art in the Dark" drawing technique. She explained, "This was a strategy utilized to motivate students to look quickly and respond by drawing their impressions of flashing lights, sounds and color in a darkened room. As a young girl I found this experience fascinating and later adapted the process in teaching my high school art classes."

Irene recalled that one of the most notorious events on the University of Georgia campus occurred in 1954. Chicago sculptor, Abbott Pattison, was commissioned by the university to create several sculptures for the campus. One of the sculptures was an Iron Horse out of sheet metal. It was at least 12 feet tall and was the first welded sculpture on the university campus. The sculpture was placed in a highly visible spot on campus and within hours a near riot broke out as students protested the abstract horse form as "too modern," unworthy of being called "art." The sculpture was removed before it was further damaged and installed on a hillside outside Athens (Van Der Kloot, 1981).

The Dodd home was often filled with interesting visitors. Influential guests such as art historians John Gardner and Jay Carter Brown; art educator Victor D'Amico; poet Robert Frost; Eileen deKooning; a group of Russian exchange artists; and many of her father's friends and artists from the New York Ashcan school were among the most memorable (personal communication, March 7, 1998).

While at the University of Georgia Irene observed and assisted Frank Wachoviak several times during his Saturday children's classes. She was particularly impressed by his sensitive discourse with each child and his motivating questioning strategies. She explained (personal communication, March 7, 1998),

> Wachoviak would not instruct in a directive manner, but he would rather raise questions like "what kind of environment does this thing operate in" or "what are the differences you can think of between these objects?" He would move around the classroom or students would come up and ask him questions, but he wasn't trying to direct them into a certain style or result as much as trying to get them involved with the process, so they were excited about what they were doing. One time just prior to the Christmas holidays a young boy was painting a large round orange circle near the center of his paper. There were other colors and shapes filling the page, even though it was unclear what was represented, it was a pleasing composition. Wachoviak proceeded around the room asking students about their work and guiding them to consider ways to improve their paintings. When he approached the young boy he made a positive comment about the overall composition of

the work, then paused and asked the boy if he would like to tell him what his painting was about. The boy nodded and pointing to the orange sphere explained it was "round young Virgin" assuming everyone was familiar with the Christmas story. Frank and I looked at each other and Wachoviak nodded in understanding, never correcting the child's interpretation of the visual image or story. He was very respectful of children. I always tried to bring that same kind of respect for students to my teaching.

Other workshop experiences, with such teacher/artists as Jacob Lawrence, Irene says, taught her "to encourage and accept differences in herself and others." Ben Shahn was not one of Irene's teachers, but she did meet him shortly before his death, at the Skowhegan Painting School in Maine. She was still a young artist and Shahn went out of his way to come to her studio to see her work. She recalls that his positive comments taught her a great deal about "the value of caring and encouragement in the life of a young artist" (personal communication, March 7, 1998).

Irene Dodd: Artist and Teacher

Although well established as a painter, with a regional and national exhibition record, Irene Dodd has taught 31 years in the state of Georgia and understands the sometimes conflicting roles of artist and teacher (personal communication, March 7, 1998).

I've had people tell me I am a good professional artist, and I'd be even better if I didn't spend to much of my time teaching…and I understand what they're talking about, but I don't think that's true in my case. I think my teaching helps my art. It takes a tremendous amount of energy to do a good job teaching; and there are only so many hours in a day, so there is less energy to devote to painting at the end of each day. Yet for me, my art and my teaching are all interrelated. If there's something you've experienced, even through your artwork, you are continually teaching about it. There is not a line that divides my social or personal life from my life as an artist, it's all interrelated. When I go out socially I often find myself talking about art or art history, and its not so much different than in teaching my classes. I'm not such a proponent of encouraging people to become artists. I try to encourage students to discover

Irene Dodd, "Gondolas," watercolor, 22" x 15", 1994

what it is that interests them. Sometimes I tell people they have a talent that they could develop if they want to pursue it. Teaching art is not an easy calling. Unfortunately it can be an easy vocation. I think some people can obtain degrees and enter a field that they really aren't suited for...sometimes the spirit isn't there for teaching, and then it just becomes dry bones....Does a person have to be a practicing artist to be a good teacher is another matter....I think in any field a creative person needs to be active and productive, but its really asking too much of a person to keep up with all the paper work and administrative duties we have now in schools, teach all day and then produce art work professionally at night. That's asking for some type of Renaissance person that at this point our system is not set up to accommodate. The energy that students produce is what feeds a creative teacher. When the average students "gets it" and lights up that's the thing that's exciting. I've seen some art teachers that are not motivated by that interaction. That's why I say it's a calling. If you're not born with the desire to teach you at least have to have an innate desire to make those deep connections with students, and communicate something about yourself or your subject matter. Sometimes you have to get into the classroom before you discover that. I don't mean you should go all the way through a degree program before you decide that either. I tell students to get out in the classroom...you have to understand the teaching process and how to communicate at any level. Whether it is Frank Wachoviak, or a science or math teacher the process is the same. At certain ages, in the elementary and secondary schools, more discipline and management issues may arise, and some students are hard to motivate. If it's not worth seeing even a few pupils get excited about what they're learning, then you're always going to feel a lack of fulfillment about what you're doing.

As we concluded our interview, Irene (personal communication, March 7, 1998) reminded me that while she had taken courses in art education, and taught in the public schools, her father never really saw the distinction between art and art education.

He saw the bigger picture of the artist educating the community. He didn't require that his faculty become involved in that kind of activity (art advocacy), but he saw that as his mission. You have to remember that although he developed a wonderful art education program at the university, he had never had any art education classes himself. He had grown-up with the attitude that you learn about things by getting out and gathering first-hand information, so I traveled with him to other universities, community art agencies, and museums from here to San Diego to learn how a variety of programs worked.

Lamar Dodd was an untiring advocate for art and art education in Georgia and across the South. He offered art as a new means of seeing the "truth in things" and wanted to make it accessible to everyone (Arthur, 1996). In a nonobtrusive way Lamar had sparked his passion for art in his daughter Irene and she continues to inspire her students and community. I came away from my interview with Irene Dodd with a new understanding of the history of art education in Georgia and an affirmation that perhaps the most profound testimony for art education is created on a daily basis through the relationships we forge with those closest to us, our families, students and communities.

References

Arthur, E.A. (Ed.). (1996). *Lamar Dodd: The C.L. Morehead, Jr. Collection.* Athens: GA: C.L. Moreland, Jr.

Dodd. I. (1953-54). *Journal, Vol. II: November 21, 1953-March 4, 1954.* Unpublished manuscript not submitted for publication.

Dodd, I. (1954). *Journal, Vol. III: March 4- May 20, 1954.* Unpublished manuscript not submitted for publication.

Eiland, W.U. (1996). *The truth in things: The life and career of Lamar Dodd.* Athens and London: University of Georgia Press.

Lamar Dodd: In an un-Bohemian way he sparks an art movement in the South. (September 26, 1949). *Life, 27,* 62-67.

McCutheon, E. & Nix, W.R. (1987). A brief history of the department of art.

(Unpublished paper, University of Georgia).
Van Der Kloot, W. (producer). (1981). *The iron horse*. (Video) Atlanta: Education Through Visual Works, Inc.

chapter

4

Car Art & Cruise In: A Tour Through Community Culture

Kathleen Keys and Christine Ballengee Morris

In this chapter the successes, impacts, and unexpected challenges of community-based practices are explored in an art exhibition and event, *Car Art & Cruise In*. For the past 3 years, the Ohio State University (OSU)-Newark Art Gallery in Newark, Ohio has made community-based practices a priority. In addition to affirming Ohio's car cruising culture, this project was inspired by an awareness of a growing nation-wide interest in transforming cars into art. The book and documentary film, *Wild Wheels* (Blank, 1994) exploring several national artists and art cars were used as a resource for this exhibition.

Establishing connections between new audiences, stressing the importance of car collecting, and affirming the existence of art in daily life were also aspirations. Local resources were utilized, partnerships were formed, and other community connections occurred. Community responses and involvement are measured against established community-based curatorial and management practices to determine the overall success of this project.

In the context of this exhibit and event, community-based curatorial practices are defined by Keys (1998) as organized and conscious attempts to represent, reach out to, and include community values, cultures, interests, and traditions in the curation and exhibition of visual arts. Community-based management practices are defined as utilizing talents, interests and preferences of local human resources. These resources include any combination of community members, students, faculty, and arts organization staff and the collaboration of these players to create ownership, empowerment, and responsibility among diverse individuals and groups for arts exhibitions and programming (p. 7).

This type of community-based work requires significant outreach to new audiences. These audience-building methods should also include extensive outreach to multiple cultures and communities. Arts organizations:

> should always extend to and include the artists and art of the ethnically and culturally diverse, their external programming should be relevant to and reflective of the populations they serve, their internal hierarchies should represent the full diversity of their communities, and they must establish open lines of communication with the populations they serve, forming new partnerships and making new efforts to reach out. (Nicholson as cited in Yeun, 1990, p. 93)

OSU-Newark's art gallery, in a rural community has attempted to address and explore several questions in its ongoing community-based work. Is there an existing arts community in Newark on which to build new audiences? How can the gallery help local communities to learn more about the arts? Most importantly, exhibitions such as *Car Art & Cruise In,* which are community-based, have allowed for re-examination of gallery mission and role of this university art gallery.

This descriptive and narrative case-study of *Car Art & Cruise In* exemplifies the successes achieved by utilizing community-based practices for an art exhibition and its impact on the community audience. The progression of the exhibition and event through description, an explanation of goals, community involvement, and outcomes are presented, and unexpected curatorial and management planning limitations are addressed.

Community-Based Practices

The importance and success of implementing community-based curatorial practices was evident in the exhibition, *Boats, Bait and*

Fishing Paraphernalia: A Local Folk Aesthetic. Art education researchers Blandy and Congdon (1988) organized an exhibition, which focused on local fishing culture in the Bowling Green, Ohio area. Opening in February 1987 in the School of Art Gallery at Bowling Green State University, the exhibition included objects used and collected by local fishers of the Northwest Ohio waters. Community experts in folklore, folk art, art education, art, fishing, taxidermy, model boat building, rod making, net making, fly tying and lure making (p. 242-243) were invited to help curate the exhibit.

> [Their] task was to produce an exhibit of largely handmade objects heretofore widely acknowledged as pleasing by fishers but unrecognized as art. Other purposes included attracting a new audience to the School of Art Gallery, suggesting new ways of encouraging aesthetic contemplation, supporting a community based aesthetic and recognizing art in daily living (p. 245).

Blandy and Congdon (1988) recommend that art educators work in partnerships with members of the community where they want to address artistic issues of common interest stating that "research into the informal and formal critical and appreciative structures which exist within communities needs to be undertaken" (p. 249). Support of those informal and formal critical and appreciative structures has been part of the reasoning for several of the OSU-Newark Art Gallery exhibitions and a contrast to fine arts and institutional traditions.

Careful attention has diligently been assigned to representing the multiple cultures, subcultures, communities and places in the Newark area. The gallery has also turned the tables on oppression by making a potentially exclusive system more inclusive. Traditional boundaries are continually weakened by the exhibition and representation of diverse voices who speak through the modes of visual arts and exhibition processes in the gallery space.

Redefining American culture, as described in *American Canvas* (Larson, 1997), includes suggestions for artists and communities such as: taking a second look at cultural resources that exist in local communities, looking more closely at "pockets of creativity" in our areas, attempting to bridge the needs of the professional arts sector with attempts to "involve citizens more directly in the arts, through a range of outreach, educational, and participatory activities," and lastly, this call recommends that "Instead of simply inviting citizens to attend the arts, [finding] new ways in which artists and arts organizations can bring art to the people, interacting with the public outside the concert hall, and museum [or gallery]" (Larson, 1997, p. 163).

Community-based practices need to be explored, broadened and planned more carefully to ensure the involvement of audience more directly in all phases of the arts and arts organizational processes through extensive outreach, educational, and participatory activities. An organizational extension of these practices is to constantly challenge the traditions of the art world and to find new and inventive ways to present, study and contemplate arts and culture. Encouraging first time visitors and expanding the participation levels of repeat visitors through new and creative community-based practices should also continue to be a key goal.

> In enshrining art within the temples of culture—the museum, the concert hall, the proscenium stage—we may have lost touch with the spirit of art: its direct relevance to our lives. In building an intricate network of public and private support, the thousands of institutions over the past four decades, we may have stressed the specialized, professional aspects of the arts at the expense of their more pervasive, participatory nature. In the process, art became something that we watch other people do, usually highly skilled professionals, rather than something we do ourselves (Larson, 1997, p. 59).

Taking into consideration the research of Blandy and Congdon (1988) and Larson (1997) the following goals framed the development and analysis of *Car Art & Cruise In*:

> • to organize and facilitate an indoor and outdoor community event, a cruise in, equipped with food, live music, door prizes, and trophies;
> • to gather and exhibit art work in several media from local and regional artists related to cars, made out of car parts, or about the love people have for cars;
> • to celebrate the exhibition, participating visual artists, cruisers, and the communities' love for cars;
> • to encourage an aesthetic examination of the artistry of car design

and car collecting and to recognize the existence of art in daily life in the tangible form of cars;
• to provide interactive art making projects for the event partici pants;
• to include community values, interests, and traditions in this exhibition and event under the direction of community-based practices; and
• to bridge a connection between the art gallery and the new audi ences of car artists, cruisers, and spectators.

Description

The OSU-Newark Art Gallery is an open-space art gallery housed in the classroom and faculty office building, LeFevre Hall. The gallery is open within the building's structure and in a fairly high traffic area. A "cruise in" is an event for which car enthusiasts shine up their automo-biles, travel to a designated area, register, park and then cruise the area admiring other cars, taking pictures and meeting folks with similar interests. Car enthusiasts and car collectors gather at cruises in large public places. Often there are three or more cruises a week in Ohio. On the sunny afternoon of October 18, 1997, 95 cars drove out to the gallery, registered and were part of *Car Art & Cruise In.* (See Figure 1) Aware that trophies would be awarded later in the afternoon, owners shined up their automobiles for the occasion. Many veteran cruisers and their families sat on blankets, lawn chairs and portable and col-lapsible plastic picnic tables transported to the site in their trunks. Joining the usual cruisers was a community person, independent of the cruise in tradition, who took part by decorating her own registered mini-van on site with colorful and temporary vinyl adhesive.

A multi-layered partnership was organized with a local Newark school, Cherry Valley Elementary. Cherry Valley was accustomed to running its own cruise in each Spring and was excited to partner with the gallery. The Parent Teacher Association (PTA) of Cherry Valley helped with the logistical running of the car show, registered cars, ensured that liability releases were signed, sold raffle tickets for door prizes and organized and directed the judges, panel which consisted of the OSU-Newark Dean, PTA members, students, and artists.

A food truck was contracted and fair-style food was made available.

Figure 1: The cruise in on the Newark campus.

An oldies band was booked because music is a very important part of the "cruise in" culture. The band was set up near the cruise cars and interactive artworks, forming a bridge into the gallery space. OSU-Newark college students from an art education class installed the indoor exhibition. The students opted for a more relaxed studio style accentuating the eclectic style of the exhibition.

All the pieces inside the gallery were to be made from car parts, or were to be about cars, about the love people have for cars, which included images of cars, or relating to cars in some way. The works were created by artists from Ohio or from other close regional areas. Walking into the gallery, the first piece you saw was *Auto History* by Bernard Williams, representing different types of transportation through history. *BLAM*, a front end of a car was mounted onto a gallery wall with a constructed neon shape reminiscent of a cartoon crash. (See Figure 2.) Fourth grade students from Cherry Valley created fantasy cars from recyclable materials such as used cardboard, plastic, styrofoam, and wire. Thirteen of these wonderful pieces, plus collage drawings from Cherry Valley second graders, were included in the exhibition and enabled us to mesh and present work by professional artists intermingled with art created by children and student artists.

Richard Warner, a local car enthusiast set up a display of his car

Figure 2: Car Art exhibition title wall featuring Scott Volzer's BLAM

paraphernalia collection and was available to discuss his collection. This included hundreds of antique license plates, car related signage and advertisements he has collected over the years. Several of Warner's signage and antique license plates were interspersed with the artworks on the gallery walls.

Further bridging the art of the gallery with the artistic nature of the cars outside, we curated specifically related and interactive outdoor car art pieces. An exhibition specific piece by OSU graduate student, Scott Volzer consisted of a non-running 1967 Cadillac El Dorado Convertible painted gold and transformed into a living room. Volzer utilized a TV, rug, couch, lamps, vases, and other living room accessories in the seating area of the car to create this piece entitled *House for Sale*. Some cruisers and families had their picture taken in the piece.

Another interactive piece of the exhibit was a donated used car from a local car dealership. Ramona Moon, a car artist, featured in *Wild Wheels* was hired as an artist-in-residence for the event to help children and adults decorate and turn this car into a piece of artwork. (See Figure 3.) Throughout the day, the steel surfaces of this '87 Nissan were completely covered with toys from restaurant kids' meals, junk, playing cards, kitchen utensils, silk flowers, plastic beaded necklaces, dolls, odds and ends found at thrift shops, and paint. At first, people were very hesitant to glue items to the automobile or to paint it. Eventually, people worked on the car and it soon swelled with toys and

Figure 3: Guest artist, Ramona Moon working on the interactive art car.

plastic flowers as children danced to the band. The new car artists even painted and decorated the automobile's wheels, and one tire exclaimed in paint and playing cards to viewers to, "Have a nice day!"

Near the end of the event the judges' votes were tallied, trophies were awarded and the completely decorated art car was raffled off. Several people wanted to know when the gallery would be having the next car art and cruise event? Would it be next year or sooner? Many business cards were exchanged with offers of assistance for the next event.

Analysis

As evidenced by the above description, several of the goals framing *Car Art & Cruise In* were not met—goals such as the organization and facilitation of a community event, the provision of interactive artmaking projects, the gathering and exhibition of artwork in related to cars, and the celebration of the artists and participants. Prior to the event we established a 10-car success criteria. We were pleased with the final count of 95 registered cars and over 300 people in attendance.

The goal to encourage an aesthetic examination of the artistry of car design and car collecting and to recognize the existence of art in daily life in the tangible form of cars, manifested itself in several ways. The event created discussion among participants about the unexpected connection between an art exhibition and cruises, the exhibition of car-related artwork in general, and the exploration and validation of cars as art. It was noted that six different and unexpected artistic production categories existed within this event. The first category was the traditionalist car artist who refinishes automobiles to achieve their total and complete original appearance. The second category included a more flexible traditionalist who uses new colors of auto paint or changes the format of the car in some way. Third, there were those who decorate a new car with a temporary application of a design. The fourth category were those who completely transform a working automobile into an art object. Fifth were those who incorporate some other visual art element into the presentation of their car such as, installations of pretend passengers, drive-in food trays, sticks of cotton candy, a showcase of trophies and awards in a trunk, or small models of their car within the car. Sometimes things were hand painted or airbrushed onto the car, under the hood, or on the bumper. Finally, the sixth category included visual artists and students who work in both traditional and new media.

Multiple community connections were developed between individuals, students, Cherry Valley Elementary, and a local car dealership. These connections fulfilled the priority of applying community-based practices including the successful portrayal of community values, interests, and traditions. Connecting car artists, cruisers, and spectators through the instigation and organization of the event embraced specific community values, interests and traditions as well as invited and introduced the art gallery to a new audience of car cruisers and their families. The results of ownership and responsibility, as demonstrated by the great interest in future similar events, was overwhelming and also evidence that our community-based goals had been met.

The positioning of the entire event was also important. Activities were both outside and inside, linking both the cruising cars to the band and to the entrance of the gallery. The architectural placement of the restrooms near the gallery serendipitously brought in several additional visitors who may have otherwise not wandered into the gallery.

This project revealed several positive outcomes from community-based practices, but also brought our attention to unexpected curatorial and management planning challenges. We learned new things about these practices, their limitations, and how to better apply them in the future. Although the initial goals of the exhibition and event were met, additional outcomes incurred by some participants were overlooked. Moon's artistic expertise and Warner's savvy collecting were rewarded by honorariums, Volzer's interactive piece was judged only for exhibition admittance, and the on-site vinyl decorating of a participants registered mini-van went unacknowledged. This latter participant approached us and commented on the need for validation of these unexpected community guided outcomes. As curators and managers of the exhibition and event, we emphatically celebrated the cruisers with trophies but failed to recognize the contributions of other community members. There was not an original car art category, nor were there categories for awarding the visual art pieces with ribbons or trophies. We had asked the campus Dean, students, artists, and members of the PTA to judge the cruisers and their artistic contributions, but did not ask the cruisers to judge or voice their opinions about anything.

We learned that the gallery's role as an educational resource is expanded by intense and ongoing collaboration and by building and by consistently utilizing public and participant forums for the exchange of ideas. Our development of partnerships and casual forums in our preliminary planning provided connections, but it is consistency throughout the entire process where significant ownership develops. Though we had established forums between ourselves and the different partners, these segments did not convene for the first time until the actual event.

Despite missing some connections, a certain level of community ownership of the exhibition and event were established. For example, many participants, including the owner of the mini-van, offered business cards and expressed great interest in playing a larger part in the next *Car Art & Cruise In.*

Conclusion

In addition to the aforementioned positive outcomes, a deeper and reflexive meaning occurred for the art gallery. As a result of this implementation of community-based practices, their inclusion within the gallery mission was changed from informal to formal. Prior to this, the mission of the OSU-Newark Art Gallery was to exhibit art of local, regional, national, and international artists and to serve as an arts education resource for Newark and surrounding communities. Now, the art gallery mission is to present many cultures of place through community-based exhibitions in efforts to expose greater audiences to cultures and art, to educate viewers, and to act as an arts education resource and advocate for Newark and surrounding communities. It is by the implementation of related policy that the continuation and strengthening of community-based practices and appropriate core values can be assured.

Policy provides the structure for strong community relationships, arts exposure, and arts education. By implementing community-based practices as formal policy, arts institutions are able to present the arts and culture of place, to the people in their communities. It is antici-pated that these practices and policies will provide ownership and significant arts experiences for communities, open doors to arts education, and challenge taken for granted assumptions in the arts world.

In accordance with the exploration and implementation of community-based practices, and the implementation of related policies, several challenges for arts administrators and cultural workers exist. First, it is imperative that arts administrators make strident efforts to cater to and support community interests within art organizations. Second, while striving for balance between all arts areas and working in multiple partnerships and collaborations, administrators should honor pluralist and extended goals for the arts and arts education. Third, administrators and cultural workers should be responsible for implementing innovative change, providing a futuristic vision for arts organizations, and remembering that pedagogy occurs in places other than the traditional classroom.

The potential contributions of community-based practices will assist arts organizations and educators across the nation as they try to find new ways to increase audiences, provide links with their communities, implement arts education programming, and establish policy that further impacts the communities that they are designed to serve. It is these activities, practices and policies that affirm and present the arts and cultures of a place, reject elitism and isolation in the arts, provide ownership for community members in the arts and arts related processes, and thus assist communities in seeing art as a part of daily life.

References

Blandy, D. & Congdon, K. (1988). Community-based aesthetics as exhibition catalyst and a foundation for community involvement in art education. *Studies in Art Education, 29,* 243-249.

Blank, H. (1994). *Wild wheels,* Rohnert CA: Pomegranate Artbooks.

Keys, K. (1998). *Community voices on participation, attitude & expectations, art education, role & mission and, community-based practices: A case study of The Ohio State University-Newark Art Gallery.* Unpublished master's thesis, The Ohio State University, Columbus.

Larson, G.O. (1997). *American canvas: An arts legacy for our communities.* Washington DC: National Endowment for the Arts.

Yeun, C.L. (1990). *Community vision: A policy guide to local arts agency development.* J. Fiscella & D.C. Speedie, Eds. Washington DC: The National Assembly of Local Arts Agencies.

chapter

5

Hartman's Historical Rock Garden: Learning About Art in Someone's Backyard

Karen M. Kakas

My husband and I arrived early on a mild, October morning, hoping to avoid competing with the crowds for parking places on the opening day of Kentuck, the annual arts and crafts festival that attracts thousands each autumn to Northport, Alabama. This year, we intended to buy another painting to add to our small collection of nontraditional folk art, a label I often use for works labeled "outsider art."[1] To our dismay, a small crowd was already surrounding Jimmy Lee Sudduth, the Black artist from Fayette, well known for his paintings made with mud and pigment on plywood. Overhearing bits of conversation, we learned that this group included two out-of-state gallery dealers, one from Memphis, another from New Orleans.[2] Nearby, Mose Tolliver, seated behind his walker, was being hovered over by other dealers. His daughter Annie's paintings, affordable to us last year, were now beyond our price range. Howard Finster was here again with his army of angels, an image he and his sons were reproducing for the growing number of folk art buyers. The scene at Kentuck revealed that art as commodity, written about with concern by Suzi Gablik (1984), had moved from the contemporary art world into the folk art world.[3] Beneath the southern pines in Kentuck Park, with the aroma of sausage and biscuits wafting from a food vendor's grill, and amid the crowds, I acquired a bit of knowledge about the art market and contemporary folk art.

Yet, one facet of this art, the folk art environment, has remained less affected by the market-driven professional art world. We can learn about art in many ways, e.g., instruction in schools, museums, and community centers; visits to museums, art galleries, and arts festivals; reading books, magazines, and newspapers; and conversations with others. However, my purpose in this chapter will be to delineate the ways art education occurs when we visit folk art environments.

The Folk Art Environment

According to SPACES (1982), the newsletter of a national organiza-tion committed to documenting and preserving such places, "Folk art environments are handmade personal places. They may be buildings, gardens, decorated walls, or accumulations of objects. No two folk environments look alike, but they are all similar in their disregard of the traditional materials, forms, and methods of architecture, painting, and sculpture"(p.1).[4] Beardsley (1995) describes them as "Part architecture, part sculpture, part landscape, visionary environments seem insistently and purposefully to defy the usual categories of artistic practice" (p. 8). These extraordinary places, which might be labeled "installations" by a New York art critic (McEvilley, 1997), are found in urban and rural areas across the United States and in other countries.   They bear such names as Prisbrey's Bottle Village (Simi Valley, California), Watts Towers (Los Angeles), MaCelle's Museum of Micellanea (Gordo, Alabama), Ave Maria Grotto (Cullman, Ala-bama), Rhinestone Cowboy House (McComb, Mississippi), Silvio Barile's Italian-American Artistic and Historical Museum (Redford, Michigan), and Hartman's Historical Rock Garden (Springfield, Ohio).[5] Before 1980, Seymour Rosen (1979) identified more than 300 large-scale creations and thousands of small environments in this country.[6] However, as more sites were discovered and documented, others were destroyed or damaged by vandalism, theft, land develop-ers, new owners of a property, and the effects of weather.

While interest in 18th and 19th century traditional American folk art grew during the first half of this century, attention was not drawn to folk art environments until the 1950s when controversy arose over Watts Towers. In 1954, after Italian immigrant Simon Rodia aban-doned his property and the construction on which he had worked for

33 years, debate ensued about whether the Towers were great art or an eyesore that might fall and destroy neighborhood property during an earthquake. Eventually, the art advocates won the debate, and the Towers were saved. In fact, delegates attending the 11th Annual International Assembly of Art Historians in 1959 drafted a resolution that claimed Watts Towers as "a unique combination of sculpture and architecture and a paramount achievement of twentieth-century folk art in the United States" (Morgan, 1984). At this time, attention was also drawn to other large-scale environments, including Clarence Schmidt's rambling seven-story structure near Woodstock, New York. By the 1960s a number of publications and exhibitions began to feature articles about and photographs of environments. For example, photographs of Watts Towers were included in the Museum of Modern Art's 1961 exhibition, "The Art of Assemblage;" in 1969, "Naives and Visionaries," a major exhibition at the Walker Art Center in Minneapolis, documented nine large-scale environments. Even major art magazines began to draw attention to art that had been previously ignored by the contemporary art world (Maizels, 1996). During the 1980s and 1990s we have witnessed a phenomenal explosion of interest in nontraditional folk art in general, evidenced by museum exhibitions, art expositions in major U.S. cities, numerous galleries, and publications that feature the art of the so-called self-taught artist.

I first learned about folk art environments more than 20 years ago when I saw a friend's photographs of a "Historical Rock Garden" she had discovered in nearby Springfield, Ohio. Seeing a small sign posted on the road leading into the outskirts of town, Judy turned onto a side street, drove a few blocks, and saw a white bungalow, a white picket fence, and a most unusual garden, a miniature world of stone and cement structures and figures. The photographs sparked my curiosity, and my first visit to Ben Hartman's Historical Rock Garden led to many others over the years and conversations with his widow Mary, who tended his garden after his death in 1944 until her move to a retirement home in 1995.[7]

People used to primarily learn about folk art environments through word of mouth or by noticing them when going to and from work, school, church, or the store. With increased publicity about them over the past 30 years, these interior and exterior spaces are now visited by

A 1962 photograph of Mary Hartman and her grandson Jeff in the north section of the Garden. Photo: Dick Shepherd, *Dayton Daily News.*

thousands who may include senior citizen tour groups, school children on field trips, family vacationers, folk art scholars, and still the curious passerby. Folk art environments attract a broad spectrum of the American public, including many who may not visit art museums and galleries or who have little or no formal art education. My experiences with these personal places, both those I visited and others I read about, have led me to believe in their value, not only for the aesthetic pleasures derived from them, but also for the informal art education they provide to visitors and the community.

Hartman's Historical Rock Garden

Before outlining the kinds of art learning I believe takes place when the public encounters folk art environments, a return to Hartman's Historical Rock Garden will set the stage. What did I find? More than 50 buildings and other structures, ranging in height from 18 inches to a 12-foot high castle, several hundred cement figures placed among numerous flower beds, and a cement picket fence bordering much of the property. I was charmed and intrigued by the diversity in this amazing place—Snow White and the Seven Dwarfs; the deer, birds, squirrels, and horses; pairs of animals lined up on the ramp to Noah's Ark; Sitting Bull and his friends, Charlie McCarthy and Mae West; a castle which, according to a didactic sign, contained 107 windows and took 14 days to build with over 10,000 stones; the unfinished Italian cathedral (the facade of his workshop), Lincoln's birthplace, the Tree of Life, and much more.[8]

Whatever Hartman enjoyed or valued became part of his garden-heroes and events in American history, patriotism, scenes from the Bible, children's nursery rhymes and storybook characters, popular culture of the 1930s, Springfield history, along with numerous animals and little people. His attitudes about war and conflict are reflected in a World War I tableau that contains injured and maimed soldiers accompanied by a small sign "The Sad Part of War," and the figure of the "Sorrowful Mother" bent over in grief. "Let it wave in peace—war is hell" is formed in glass letters on the pavement in front of Betsy Ross's house.

In the center of a flower bed stands his homage to coffee, a giant coffee cup and saucer on a pedestal. "Good to the last drop," he used to say to visitors. According to Mrs. Hartman, he was especially proud of the "Tree of Life," a 7-foot structure that resembles a saguaro cactus. In the center, an eagle rests on a globe covered with stripes of red and white stones. On top of one cactus arm sits a one-room schoolhouse and the other arm supports a church. Doves symbolizing peace sit in the crook of the arms. To Hartman, the "Tree of Life," symbolized "everything important in life—country, school, and church" (Baker, personal communication, 1992). His concern for family was reflected in groupings of animals among the flowers surrounding the tree (Few remain because of vandalism in recent years.). Family values are expressed with messages created in mosaics of broken mirrors and glass embedded in narrow cement paths, such as "Behold thy mother and don't forget your dad," and "When the rest of the world don't want you, come back to mother and dad."

What prompted a 48 year old man with no schooling beyond first grade and with no formal art education to devote the last 12 years of

HARTMAN'S ROCK GARDEN
SPRINGFIELD, OHIO

A reproduction of a 1930s postcard, one
of several photographs the Hartmans
had reproduced to sell to the public.
Photographer unknown

his life to his vision in stone and cement? In 1932, laid off from a local foundry where he worked as an iron molder making bed frames, Hartman began what would become his personal "WPA" project. Not wanting to remain idle and being an avid fisherman, he decided to build a fishing pond in his backyard. After that, using his moldmaking skills, he began to construct small buildings and other structures. Hartman used wooden forms to build up the walls of the buildings with layers of cement whose damp surfaces he covered with small stones. Over the years, he seemed to increasingly consider, aesthetically, the sizes, shapes, and colors of the stones as he planned their arrangement on the cement surfaces.

To create most of his figures, Hartman made molds from inexpensive plaster of paris statues he had purchased. At times, when recasting them in cement, he combined parts from several statues. After he painted the new sculptures, he arranged them among the buildings and flowers beds. Using this casting method, Hartman created countless storybook and radio program characters, religious figures, famous people in American history, celebrities, and animals. He also made original molds to cast forms in iron or lead, such as 5-inch tall evergreen trees.

Many scenes reveal accurate scale relationships among the objects, such as the soldiers in front of Barbara Fritchie's house, the trees and cannon next to George Washington's Headquarters, and the farm scene complete with a produce stand containing tiny vegetables. However, disinterest in scale relationships is also evident. For example, Snow

White is no taller than her dwarfs and a large cat stands on the roof of Mount Vernon. These unusual scale relationships and others evoke a whimsical charm and humor in the Garden.

As Hartman worked on the Garden, curious motorists began to stop and ask about his project. He enjoyed answering their questions, encouraged them to return, and as his Garden grew, so did the number of visitors. Hartman began to give guided tours, telling stories, some containing bits of humor, about the buildings, scenes, and figures. Sightseeing on the weekends was a popular pastime during the Depression, and on busy days his daughter Ruth and niece Gladys helped give tours. Mrs. Hartman recalled that visitors would "give him a nickel or a dime. He'd save them in his pocket until he got 50 cents—that's how much a bag of cement cost then. He'd come and say, 'Honey, get me another sack of cement.'" (M. Hartman, personal communication, 1985). After Hartman's death, intent on keeping his Garden intact, Mrs. Hartman welcomed visitors and continued to tell his stories, recounting what he had said about specific pieces.

Every visit revealed something I had not seen before—an animal, a figure, a structural detail—and I never ceased to marvel at Hartman's commitment and devotion to a project that was unfinished at the time of his death from silicosis. From my research on other folk art environments, I learned that Hartman shared several characteristics with others who have embellished their property with their personal visions. Many often began their constructions later in life, perhaps after loss of a job, a loved one, or a significant change in their lives. These creators tended to be less educated, were poor, and generally had worked in low-status jobs. They often used skills acquired at work or that they had taught themselves during the artmaking process. Inexpensive materials were typically used—cement and stone, wood, discarded objects; rummaging through the dump was not an uncommon practice (Beardsley, 1995; Manley, 1989). Expression of personal beliefs and values were important to these artists, who tended to focus on several major themes, including American history, honoring people and places, religion, family, patriotism, and popular culture.

Writing about folk art environments typically focuses on descriptions of the places and the individuals who created them. But how is the

Sitting Bull and his companions peer
intently from the "Old West" section of
the Garden. Photo: Karen Kakas

public affected by visiting these
personal places? Besides the
enjoyment, what does the novice
art viewer learn about art upon
encountering these objects in
someone's backyard? I contend
that Hartman's Historical Rock
Garden, Watts Towers, Prisbrey's
Bottle Village, and the numerous
folk art environments that dot the
American landscape provide
information about the nature of
art, artists, and the artmaking
process.

What Visitors Learn About
The Nature of Art

Significant art can exist outside
museums and art galleries, and is
not separate from people's lives
and their community. Lippard (1994) states, "So-called folk artists
tend to be more relaxed than so-called fine artists about crossing back
and forth over the borders between life and art, and about the idea that
both art objects and art making have healing powers" (p. 14).
Lippard's reference to "healing powers" reminds us that artmaking can
be therapeutic for an artist. Hartman's unemployment no doubt had
an effect on his perceptions of himself as a productive husband, father,
and member of the community. Visitors who hear Mrs. Hartman's
stories about Hartman, his intense involvement with his work, the
crowds attracted to see the Garden and talk with him, will come to
understand the value of this project to his personal identity. However,
viewing art can also have healing power. It is likely that members of
the community, many of them unemployed as well, spent an uplifting
Sunday afternoon in Hartman's Garden, listening to his stories and
humorous sayings, and marveling at his creations.

Artworks can change over time and can be impermanent. Unlike
works of art displayed in museums that are meant to be viewed as

completed entities, Hartman's Garden evolved over the years as he created more structures and figures, rearranged pieces, added signs and didactic labels. People who were repeat visitors would see art that had changed, not only because of what Hartman had added or moved, but also because of the effects of weather on his structures, and, much later, the results of vandalism.

Understanding and appreciating works of art can be enhanced by contextual information, such as titles, labels, and conversations with the artist. My perceptions of Hartman's environment were greatly affected by what I learned about his life, his working methods, his stories, his interaction with the public, as well as life in America in the 1930s. I began to appreciate his Garden not only for its visual quali- ties, but also for the beliefs and values he expressed. And I was stimulated to reflect about many of the ideas I am offering in this paper.

These places may stimulate visitors to ponder aesthetic issues about art. Are these environments "art"? Is this folk art? Are the individual parts the art? Or is the entire place the work of art? Are Hartman's figures less good as art because he used mass produced plaster statues to create his molds? Shouldn't he have been more original? On the other hand, isn't he original, because no other garden in Springfield or Ohio or America or the world looks like his? How important is originality in art? What do we mean by originality anyway?

What Visitors Learn About The Nature of Artists

Art can be made by anyone—if the person is motivated and has the desire to communicate ideas, beliefs, and values; and in doing so, makes something special that didn't previously exist. For, according to folklorist Michael Owen Jones, all people have a "feeling for form" (Ames, 1993, p. 90) that can be evident in the ways they arrange objects on a kitchen counter, in a basement workshop, or on the front porch. This feeling for form is manifested on a different level, when people make art. Moreover, art is made by many people who have no academic art education. As a teenager, Hartman learned his moldmaking from his uncle. As he experimented with placing stones and pebbles in damp cement, he became increasingly skilled, both technically and aesthetically, with the materials.

Interest in making art can occur at any time in life. Hartman was 48 years old when he created his fishing pond. Tressa Prisbrey constructed the first part of her "Bottle Village" when she was in her late 50s. After he stopped farming at age 65, Fred Smith began to build his "Concrete Park" (Sellen & Johanson, 1993). In unexpected and unforeseen ways, people start to make art. What prompts someone to pick up pieces of scrap metal in the barn and start to play around with them until it is transformed into something else? What happens during that act of creating that sparks motivation to do more until the making seems like an important job that must be done every day? Or is it the response from others that sparks that motivation? This is another aesthetic issue that viewers might ponder as they reflect on what motivates someone to make art.

Visits to several folk art environments can provide insight on the numerous ways individuals are motivated to start their constructions. Treesa Prisbrey wanted to build a house for her collection of 17,000 pencils; Hartman, unemployed and with time on his hands, decided to dig a hole for a fishing pond in his backyard. We, as visitors, may begin to sense other reasons—a desire to leave a permanent record of themselves, to express their beliefs and values to the community, to entertain family members, to avoid isolation, to socialize with people, to gain recognition, to feel satisfaction with an achievement.

Artists work very hard at what they do, spending huge amounts of time and energy. Artmaking may dominate their lives. They live their art; their art is their life. Clarence Schmidt worked every day for 30 years on his House of Mirrors. Hartman hauled and hammered countless rocks into smaller pieces for his Garden; he used a single wooden mold to create 410 pickets for his cement picket fence. Simon Rodia toiled single-handedly to build his three, enormous towers, richly encrusted with a mosaic of broken bottles and plates, seashells, and ceramic tiles (Beardsley, 1995).

Artworks reflect an artist's responses to a life lived within a specific culture, time, and place. The inception of an idea may surface from childhood memories or what has been seen, heard, or read over the years. A man who traveled very little, many of Hartman's ideas came from looking at pictures—*National Geographic* magazine, his daughter's elementary school textbooks and religious storybooks, and picture postcards. His favorite radio programs and his knowledge and views about American history were also reflected in the Garden.

What Visitors Learn About the ArtMaking Process

Art can be made from anything—scrap metal, broken pop bottles and crockery, sea shells, cement, pebbles; nature materials, and the refuse of our throwaway society. Special tools and materials are not a prerequisite for making art. Hartman and others used what was free or inexpensive, materials to which they had easy access. They weren't trying to make a statement about this; whereas, Duchamp consciously demonstrated that art could be made out of anything (Gablik, 1984). According to Gablik (1984), "There is nothing about an object—no special property or function—that makes something a work of art, except our attitude toward it, and our willingness to accept it as art" (p. 38).

The sources for some artists' work may come from previously existing objects and images (borrowing that postmodernists call "appropriating"). Hartman purchased plaster of paris statues to create molds for his cement sculptures; he bought small porcelain figures, and toy cars and soldiers for some scenes. Tressa Prisbrey used everything imaginable in her Bottle Village—bottles, hubcaps, dolls, 17,000 pencils, television picture tubes, antlers, gourds, headlights, and more.

Artists don't always work alone. They may collaborate with others on their projects. Mary Hartman worked with Hartman in many ways— she helped gather stones, made dolls for some of the interiors (such as Betsy Ross, sitting in her house and sewing the flag), planted flower beds, painted signs, and repainted sculptures. A neighbor made dollhouse-size benches to put inside the schoolhouse. Some community members offered items, such as seashells and rocks, for the Garden; someone brought a picture postcard of an Italian cathedral, which prompted Hartman to add a cathedral-like facade to his workshop.

Conclusion

My musing about what we learn when we visit art environments is not meant to be investigative reporting. In fact, I challenge others to investigate, to conduct research at such environments. Interview visitors and ask questions about their responses to these places. Are they art? What did they come away with after visiting these unique creations? What unanswered questions are on their minds? What might we learn about the ways art viewers of all kinds think about art as they reflect on their experiences at these sites?

In the mean time, I intend to plan more field trips for my art education students and to continue showing slides of environments and other art that is not typically introduced to them in art history survey and twentieth century courses. Future teachers of art who will have impact on young students' conceptions of art need to broaden their own conceptions of art, the nature of artists, and the artmaking process. As postmodernism is breaking down the hierarchical distinctions that have been traditionally made about artworks, our students, who often continue to be taught from a modernist perspective in studio courses (Dunning, 1998), must be introduced to the diversity of art that exists outside of the professional/fine art world. Our students ought to learn that "as multiculturalism has rendered the notion of a static, cultural mainstream forever problematic, the pathway has been opened for a more inclusive understanding of what constitutes significant art" (Borum, 1994, p.3).

In addition, we need to make our students aware that most environments are like an endangered species. For without our efforts to protect and preserve them, we will lose many, if not most, to extinction. These losses would be a sad reminder that most resources for such efforts are focused on art objects housed in museums. Moreover, when environments are lost, "communities are diminished. They lose not only diversity, and visual and folkloric stimulation, but also community focus and sometimes spiritual sustenance" (Manley, 1994).

The more I reflect and teach about this topic, the less I seem to use "folk" in my discussion, a sign that I, an art educator taught from a modernist perspective in my undergraduate and graduate days, am beginning to think about art without using labels that suggest polarities. Yet, McEvilley (1997) realistically concluded, "The seemingly intractable question of terminology is far from being resolved, and one suspects that it may never be, as long as the inequalities of the society at large have not been addressed" (p. 85).

I want us not to forget the joy and satisfaction that arises when Hartman and others create their gardens, environments, visionary spaces, yard art, and yard shows. Treesa Prisbry, in reference to her Bottle Village said, "Anyone can do anything with a million dollars—look at Disney. But it takes more than money to make something out of nothing, and look at the fun I have doing it" (Beardsley, 1995, p.7). Nor should we lose sight of how these environments provide rich evidence of the human urge to create. And finally, Rosen's statement can be instructive to us all, "What seems to make these people different is that they took their dreams, made the time to do something about them" (1979, p. 162). For as art viewers and art educators, we ought to take time to discover, explore, appreciate, and help preserve these extraordinary places.

Endnotes

[1]The label "outsider" is one of many being used by critics, collectors, museums, gallery dealers, and publications as they attempt to categorize and give a name to the art of individuals who were not educated in the art school tradition. "Self-taught," "folk," "intuitive," "visionary," "vernacular," and "naive" are also prominent contenders. Throughout the 1990s debate ensued in many art circles about these categorizing and labeling attempts. The September 1994 issue of *New Art Examiner* was devoted to this topic, and more recently, Thomas McEvilley (1997) provided insightful remarks about this issue.

[2]Jimmy Lee Sudduth's paintings are sold in as many as 49 galleries throughout the country (Sellen & Johanson, 1993).

[3]Howard Becker's (1982) social theory of art makes distinctions among multiple art worlds in contrast to the traditional view of one art world, which refers to the professional/fine art world.

[4]Other labels used for these constructed spaces include "yard art" (Sheehy, 1998); "visionary environments" (Maizel, 1996); "yard show" (McEvilley, 1997), referring to African-American creations; and, finally, "environment" (Beardsley, 1995).

[5]Among the publications that feature artists' environments, several are excellent sources of information and photographs: *Gardens of Revelation* (Beardsley, 1995), *Raw Creation* (Maizel, 1996), chapters on a selection of environments in *Self-made Worlds* (Manley & Sloan, 1997), and *Naives and Visionaries* (1974). *Raw Visions*, an international journal on self-taught artists, is another valuable resource.

[6]In 1979, California photographer Seymour Rosen founded SPACES, an acronym for Saving and Preserving Arts and Cultural Environments. To obtain the organization's newsletter, write to SPACES, 1804 N. Van Ness, Los Angeles, CA 90028.

[7]After Mary Hartman moved to a retirement home in 1994, her son Ben moved back to the family home to maintain the Garden. Interviews with Mrs. Hartman and photographs of the Garden taken in the 1980s were included in a *Columbus Art* article (Kakas, 1985). Additional research was conducted in the early 1990s for a traveling exhibition, "Hartman's Historical Rock Garden: One Man's Vision Cast in Stone," which featured photographs by the author and others, a video, and catalog.

[8]A detailed account of Hartman and his Garden can be found in the catalog, which accompanied the exhibit cited in Note 7. A limited number are available and can be obtained by contacting the author, School of Art, Bowling Green State University, Bowling Green, OH 43403.

References

Ames, Kenneth L. (1993). Folk art and cultural values. *In Common ground/ uncommon vision; The Michael and Julie Hall collection of American folk art* (pp. 83-93). Milwaukee: Milwaukee Art Museum.

Beardsley, J. (1995). *Gardens of revelation: Environments by visionary artists*. NY: Abbeville Press.

Becker, H. (1982). *Art worlds*. Berkeley: University of California Press

Borum, J.P. (1994, September). Editorial. *New Art Examiner*, 3-4.

Dunning, W.V. (1998). *Advice to young artists in a postmodern era*. Syracuse, NY: Syracuse University Press.

Gablik, S. (1984). *Has modernism failed?* NY: Thames & Hudson.

Kakas, K. (1985). Hartman's historical rock garden. *Columbus Art, 6*(4), 5-6.

Lippard, L. (1994). Crossing into uncommon grounds. In M.D. Hall & E.W. Metcalf, Jr. (Eds.) *The artist outsider: Creativity and the boundaries of culture* (pp. 3-18). Washington, DC: Smithsonian Institution Press.

Maizels, J. (1996). *Raw creation: Outsider art and beyond*. London: Phaidon Press.

Manley, R. & M. Sloan. (1997). *Self-made worlds: Visionary folk art environments*. NY: Aperture.

Manley, R. (1994, September). Collecting with concern for the (self-taught) environment. *New Art Examiner,* 35-36.

Manley, R. (1989). *Signs and Wonders: Outsider art inside North Carolina.* Raleigh, NC: North Carolina Museum of Art.

McEvilley, T. (1997, May). The missing tradition. *Art in America, 85*(5), 78-85, 137.

Morgan, J. (1984). Rodia's towers: Nuestro Pueblo, a gift to the world. In D. Ward (Ed.) *Personal places: Perspectives on informal art environments* (pp. 72-82). Bowling Green, OH: Bowling Green State University Popular Press.

Naives and visionaries. (1974). Minneapolis: Walker Art Center; New York: E.P. Dutton.

New Art Examiner. (1994, September).

Rosen, S. (1979). *In celebration of ourselves.* San Francisco: California Living Books.

Sellen, B.C. & Johanson, C.J. (1993). *20th century American folk, self taught, and outsider art.* NY: Neal-Schuman Publishers, Inc.

Sheehy, C.J. (1998). *The flamingo in the garden: American yard art and the vernacular landscape.* NY: Garland Publishing, Inc.

SPACES (1982). *1*,1,1.

Community as Learning Group

Seen through the chapters of this book, histories of community-based art education touch and entwine with a variety of contexts, including ethnic and family identification, as well as recognizing the importance of place within the history of art education. It is also the case that individuals and groups collectively share and shape values and beliefs in critical ways that help educate others within a given community.

The chapters in this section of the book give voice to an array of educators who have carried on their lives and work within community-based learning groups. The notion of community-based art education is very broad, and is not seen to exclude those settings where formal education occurs. Schools are a part of many, if not most local and regional communities. For this reason, some stories in this section are written about those who taught art within schools. However, the stories told in this section of the book extend art education history beyond formal educational institutions to include learning groups as being those who carry out innovative curricular and instructional programs in art education, people who work on and educate themselves and others through craft kits, and personal histories of those who have assisted self-taught artists.

Hearing the stories of others should cause us to pause and reflect on our own position in the world. What stories are woven into the fabric of who we are? What tales from our past have shaped and continue to form our lives today? The following narratives about community as learning group add a rich and much overlooked quality to art education and to ourselves.

Paul E. Bolin
Co-Editor

chapter

7

Personal Histories of Artists Who Assisted Prominent Self-Taught Artists

Jean Ellen Jones

The artwork of self-taught artists in the United States first received wide recognition in the 1970s and 1980s. Operating at the confluence of the self-taught and mainstream art worlds was the person I will call the assistant, who befriended the artist and often played a major role in getting the artist's work known. Most of the recognized artists had one or more assistants. For example, of the 20 self-taught artists included in the seminal Corcoran Gallery Show, "Black Folk Art in America: 1930-1980," 16 had special friends whom exhibition organizers Livingston and Beardsley (1982) acknowledged for working with the artists.

Activities of some assistants have since been reported in the media, where the assistants are nearly always portrayed as controversial figures (Fager, 1993; Vesey, 1993). Most assistants have received little attention. Newspaper reporters and art historians writing about the self-taught art field usually mention the name of an assistant, if at all, in a sentence or two and then focus on the artist. Having been one of these assistants, and recognizing that there is much more to the relationship than has received attention in the popular or scholarly press, I have undertaken a study of the assistant role. This chapter examines some of what I have found through my study of these assistants.

Method

The focus of the study was assistants who worked with 15 recognized self-taught artists. To be considered an assistant, a person had to have developed a primary and long-term relationship with one or more of the artists. The study included interviews with over 30 assistants. Recognized self-taught artists were selected from among persons who had received positive critical attention from the art world during the 1970s and 1980s and been represented in at least two Museum-sponsored exhibitions. A very large number of such self-taught artists were from the Southeast and Midwest United States.

Interviews with the assistants included a structured set of guiding questions and exploration of issues important to the assistants. Questions moved from the assistants' life history to details of their experience as assistants and then to reflection on the meaning of the experience for them and the self-taught artist. Most interviews took place in two separate sessions for a total of about three hours.

As the study unfolded, a high proportion of academically-trained artists turned up in the assistants group. Thirteen of 30 were artists. Almost all of the self-taught artists had attracted at least one artist assistant. Traditionally artists are discovered and promoted by gallery owners, museum directors, or art critics, not by other artists. The academically-trained artists' involvement with self-taught artists seems to be one manifestation of an ever-broadening interest in diverse art forms in the late 20th century. Their involvement may also signal a broadening of the path through which an artist's work becomes known, taking the role of such self-taught art promoters as Dubuffet to a new dimension. This chapter provides an overview of the artist assistants' story. While acknowledging the new historical information that the study may reveal, this analysis will focus on educational implications, outlining how the study may instruct a wide range of persons in community settings who develop art-centered relationships every day.

Profiles of Artist Assistants

The 13 artists who surfaced as important assistants to the selected prominent self-taught artists had studied art through art schools and university art departments. Six had MFA degrees, 6 had BFA degrees, and 1 had taken the equivalent of a BFA at recognized institutions. All had continued to make art professionally following graduation. Nearly all of the artist assistants were Caucasian and from middle class to upper class socioeconomic backgrounds, while nearly all of the self-taught artists were African American and from rural, low socioeconomic backgrounds.

Background of Artist Assistants

Biographies of the artist assistants reveal an early fascination with self-taught art and persons outside their cultural group of origin. They speak of being drawn to roadside tourist attractions, car art, and tattoo design. When the interviewer asked one artist assistant to tell about his childhood, he said,

> To the back [of my neighborhood] were blacks. And when I was very, very young, I was always fascinated because the kids would come up the streets, the black kids, with these homemade scooters made out of...two-by-fours, or cast off wood, and I was always fascinated. I wanted one so bad. They were covered with bottle caps, and the wheels were old skates...And back then, too, there was always a black guy who had a truck, selling vegetables. He'd just slowly come down the road. And it, too, was all decorated with paint and things, and bottle caps. You know, it was just like fascinating. It was sort of like the equivalent of those taxis you see in the Philippines.

Another artist recalled, when she was 7 or 8,

> getting a *101 Dalmatians* coloring book and coloring everybody black in the book, for two reasons. One, the black crayon was the sharpest and pointiest, and so, that was the crayon I wanted to use, but also, I was, I think at that point, was really becoming conscious of differences, and so decided well, why did everybody in the book have to be white. Why couldn't they be black?

(The black figures drew a reprimand from her mother.) This artist, who was traveling in the Third World while still in college, observed, "I gave a lot of value to other cultures...Everything seemed a lot more exciting somewhere else." Three artist assistants described important encounters with nearby self-taught artists while they were teenagers and young adults. Others became interested in self-taught art through contact with enthusiastic professors at Midwestern university art departments.

Getting Together

Typically, a friend or colleague told the artist assistant about the self-taught artist. They knew the artist assistant was "always drawn to kind of eccentric things," or was interested in exhibiting or documenting the work of local artists, or might be interested just because he or she was an artist. The meeting was a life-altering event for most artist assistants: "He had unbelievable energy…and this guy just had art everywhere. I mean, he was just painting up a storm and nobody cared, nobody." Another said, "It was like opening up the tomb of Egypt. I couldn't believe how his artwork resonated with an abstract, primitive representation." Many of the artists reported a feeling of personal connection: "I immediately fell in love with him, and liked him, and liked his work, and really was able to speak to him…just as a friend."

The experience for the artist was like going on a blind date that worked. Nearly all of the self-taught artists had been visited by other artists and passersby. Likewise, nearly all of the artist assistants had met a number of self-taught artists. This time the "chemistry" was right. As a bonus, the self-taught artists were "geographically desirable." They lived as close as three blocks and usually no more than a two-hour drive from the artist assistant.

Personal Connections

Over time the relationship became as one between equals, or nearly so. The artist assistant offered more education and a presence from a more powerful cultural group; the self-taught artist brought valued personal qualities and a unique mind that the artist admired greatly. Over half of the artist assistants mentioned documentation as an important part of their role. One artist's description of his role as "fan" was true for most of the others as well. Several artist assistants told how they were deeply touched when the self-taught artist said they admired or appreciated them.

All artists described the self-taught artist as a friend. Relationships lasted over 20 years in some cases. There seemed to be three different types of friendship relations. **Presenters** visited and engaged the self-taught artist in talk about the art. Their relationship focused on a strong appreciation of the art, on the self-taught artist as an interesting person, and the organization of a first exhibition. Following that, life circumstances and the appearance of another advocate for the self-taught artist limited their contact. They followed the career of the self-taught artist mostly from afar.

A second group of artist assistants, the **helpers**, felt drawn to the self-taught artist, and helped the artist professionally and personally. On the professional side, they arranged for important galleries to handle the work, bought work, advised them about how to operate in the art world, and worked to make sure the self-taught artist's work was preserved and known after the self-taught artist's death. During visits, which occurred every week to every month or two, they encouraged the self-taught artist, engaged the self-taught artist in conversation about their work, and watched the self-taught artist work. On the personal side, they would help with house repairs, introduce the self-taught artist to friends, bring family by to visit on a Sunday afternoon, and accompany them on out-of-town trips. They would listen to stories and life philosophies and make small talk, for example: "We [would] just go and hang out in his room, and watch TV, and eat ice cream and stuff." If a self-taught artist died, their artist assistant friend usually attended the funeral. Some noted that they and a companion or two were the only persons from outside the self-taught artist's community in attendance.

The third group of artist assistants, the **seekers**, engaged in the same types of activities as the helpers, but developed a more reciprocal relationship. They received a kind of therapy from the self-taught artist. When the pressures of work or home became too much, the artist would "escape" or "hide out" at the self-taught artist's studio. One artist said that after a day of dealing with the art world, it was fun to drop in on the self-taught artist after supper and "just wash, wash out your system...and deal with a regular person." The self-taught artist became a counselor: "We were genuinely friends, and he would give me advice on all kinds of matters." Another said, "If I ever got too strung out, I could spend about two hours with [the artist] and man, everything would get into perspective so fast." They talked about spiritual matters: One artist confided that "The closest thing I could find to God or prayer was these people."

Professional Connections

The artist assistants' admiration of self-taught art led them in several directions. A few gave examples of how contact with the self-taught artists directly influenced what they made and even led to joint exhibitions. One related that as a result of contact with the self-taught artist, he experienced

> a complete change, and everything, and I really started digging deep and unconsciously came out with this outpouring of all this artwork. And it was very much like—very primitive. The things I really liked, the things that were important to me, and that turns out to be very archetypal imagery. Which is what a lot of this [imagery] of [the self-taught artist] is. And in the early days, because I liked his work, I wanted to show my work with his, to show the connection.

Many of the artists did not thrive as artists during the most intense period of their involvement with the self-taught artist. One said, "I couldn't paint for a while because I thought, 'It's useless.' Instead, he and others got caught up in documenting and promoting the art. The art of a large group of artist assistants did not in any way resemble the work of the self-taught artists. Many worked in totally different media.

The self-taught artists' act of making the art fascinated all of the academically-trained artist assistants: "It encouraged me to forget about the rules and not concentrate on the materials and the techniques and that sort of thing. [It] gave me sort of license." Another artist assistant learned,

> You just gotta start working and work. And just constantly work. And I proved it to myself so many times, you know. That's when the information really comes, for yourself. That's when you start learning from yourself. And if you make a fool out of yourself, well, who cares?

Several noted that in watching the self-taught artists at work, they realized that an artist can have fun with artmaking: "That was his fun, you know, he loved it. It made him happy."

Connection to the self-taught artist moved many of the artists to develop their career as an art collector and dealer. They got tremendous pleasure just looking at the art. In contrast to the art they saw around them and even their own art, the work of the self-taught artists seemed "deeply personal," "fresh," "a new perspective," "free," and "something that a professional artist cannot achieve." One artist related how

> the best part about running the gallery was the hour before the exhibition opened when I had the place all to myself. And the windows were still covered up, and I had a fresh installation and I could stand in the room full of beautiful artwork by myself, and enjoy it.

A few artist assistants engaged in activities that helped shape the form of the art, activities that could be considered controversial by some. Two artist assistants helped with supplying "source material," photographic images of objects and art that would inspire the self-taught artist. They saw no problem with this because the self-taught artist sometimes ignored their source material and suggestions and always transformed them in a very individual way. The same was true for the art supplies they brought. Most of the supplies were used, but some never appeared on an artwork. One artist assistant tells this story:

> I'd seen where he had taken some tin, and had bent it himself, so I thought, He'd really like this [a piece of new tin the artist had found] 'cause the corrugation is already in the piece. I remember we drove by one time and he wasn't in the yard, but we left the tin in the yard and a note. We did something else and we came by later, and he was hammering out the [tin].

These few artist assistants who supported the artmaking in this more direct way insisted that not only did the self-taught artist exercise ultimate control over the product, but emphasized that they were helping the self-taught artist grow and expand on topics and in directions the self-taught artist had already established.

The majority of artist assistants encouraged the self-taught artists, brought them supplies, and made no suggestions about the form of the artwork itself. In fact, they said they wished they could have exerted more influence on the artmaking process when many of the self-taught artists started making inferior and repetitive work to keep up with public demand. The artist assistants saw their main influence to be psychological, as a friend providing support and encouragement.

On Being Successful as an Assistant

Both artist assistants and self-taught artists in this study would say that the relationship was mutually beneficial. When the interviewer asked the artist assistants what made the relationship work, love for the self-taught artist emerged as a common theme. For example, they said, "I loved her more than most people;" [we kept the relationship going through] "love, seeing the love in each other;" and, "I was interested in them as people." Another common theme was use of their knowledge from earlier cross-cultural experiences. Those experiences taught them to be good listeners and not feel compelled to "fill the air with talk," to attend closely to body language and the subtleties of self-taught artist comments, and not to impose themselves on the other. One artist assistant said that she learned from her travels that it is important to engage in authentic communication, and took her own artwork to the first meeting to encourage that. It is telling that one of the artist assistants who had the least success in his relationships said, "That's part of my failure as an art dealer...my inability to really get involved in these guy's lives."

Despite their success in establishing a meaningful personal relationship with the self-taught artists, many of the artist assistants decreased their contact as more people vied for the self-taught artist's work. The artwork of about half of the self-taught artists in the study decreased in quality, and the environment around them seemed competitive and even hostile as the work became a commodity. It is with this history in mind that artist assistants provided advice for others who might meet an unknown self-taught artist.

Their advice, in conducting the personal or professional side of the relationship, was to let the self-taught artist be in control. Here are representative examples: One said that the assistant should be engaged in "encouraging them, not trying to get them to do this or do that, but just to think positive about whatever they do so that they don't get hampered." Several artist assistants expressed this idea: "Make them feel comfortable and see what they want out of it all, and respect it. If they don't want to sell or be exposed, then leave it as it is, and just enjoy it for what it is." Another added that if the artist wanted to sell, "Tell them that they need a manager." One summarized, "Help them gain the access they want but then step aside. Because these people can really fly, you know. They really can."

The Assistant Role from an Educational Perspective

Neither the artist assistants nor the self-taught artists would say they were involved in an educational endeavor, but an examination of adult education theory reveals that their activities provide a near-classic case of how adults learn outside the formal educational system. Researchers studying the ways adults learn in everyday life describe individuals who are constantly taking on self-directed learning projects. Descriptions of these purposeful efforts to learn and grow in a particular area usually include the self-directed learner and an array of environmental circumstances and people that the learner uses to reach the learner's goal. In the case of the artist and the self-taught artist in this study, the label *self-directed learner* seems to apply to them both.

According to adult education theory, the artist assistant and the self-taught artist are both self-taught. The self-taught artists were engaged in an extended project to learn to make art for various, mostly personal, purposes. The academically trained artist assistants were working on a number of projects, including the improvement of their art, development of themselves as wise and centered persons, training their eye for art collecting, and persuading the art world that the work of self-taught artists had value.

Candy (1991, p. 199) lists several generalizations about how adults learn in a learning-project, self-directed mode. They all seem to apply to the activities of the artist assistant and self-taught artist.

1. **There is almost always a person, and usually several people,**

who assist the self-directed learner with the project. In this case, the artist and the self-taught artist were an assistant, but not the only assistant, to the other's projects.

2. **The learning is not preplanned but proceeds through a highly irregular path.** In this case both artist assistant and self-taught artist initiated or forwarded their projects through discovered resources in the environment such as an encouraging artist assistant (for the self-taught artist), and such events chance meetings in childhood or taking a course with a certain professor in art school (for the artist assistant).

3. **A person initiates a project to solve a problem in the person's life.** For the self-taught artists, it might be an accident that sent them into early retirement; for the artist assistants it could be dissatisfaction with their artwork.

4. **Most self-directed learners do not view themselves as learners.** In this case, the self-taught artists did not call themselves learners or even artists; they were simply making things. Artist assistants mentioned such roles as artist, helper, and collector.

5. **Self-directed learning usually occurs in the context of a social grouping such as family or a work group.** Most of the self-taught artists were very much a part of their community, although they received very little support for their art making. With the arrival of their new artist friend and admirers they had access to a supportive social context. Artists operated as part of an art world subculture interested in self-taught art.

Research on the characteristics of the successful learning project assistant echoes many of the artist assistants' prescriptions for success described earlier. For example, Tremblay (as cited in Candy, 1991, p. 182) found that the ideal helper is a good listener, is flexible, and does not force his or her point of view on the learner, but gives the learner ownership of the project. Research in both self-directed learning and the mentoring process emphasizes that the most important ingredient is the quality of the personal relationship. This is the dominant theme to be gleaned from the artist assistants' personal histories with self-taught artists.

Artist assistants in this study simply liked the self-taught artists and their art, and soon became the self-taught artist's fan and student. Artists rarely mentioned the fact that they had crossed considerable cultural boundaries and expended a great deal of energy and time in fostering the relationship. They were caught up in an experience that enabled them to help an exceptional artist and to tap something unique for their own needs. This mutual benefit dynamic fueled the relationship; the love and respect they held for each other kept it together. The experience is not unique to this situation, but can occur whenever individuals launch themselves into a learning project in community with others.

References

Candy, P. C. (1991). *Self-direction for lifelong learning*. San Francisco: Jossey-Bass.

Fager, J. (Executive Producer). (1993, November 21). Tin man. *60 Minutes*. New York: CBS Broadcasting.

Livingston, J., & Beardsley, J. (1982). Acknowledgments. *Black folk art in America, 1930-1980* (Exhibition Catalog). Jackson, Mississippi: University Press of Mississippi and the Center for the Study of Southern Culture.

Vesey, S. (1993, January 3). Drawn into controversy. *The Atlanta Journal and the Atlanta Constitution*, pp. A1, A10.

Kit Crafts and the People Who Make Them: A History of Pre-Packaged Pedagogy Since 1930

Faith Agostinone-Wilson

Introduction

The field of art education, for the most part, has ignored those who make mainstream crafting their primary aesthetic activity. Notions of what makes "good art" do not typically include the experiences of those who follow "how-to" crafting projects or assemble craft kits. As a result, a large portion of craft history has gone unnoticed. This is mostly due to elitist notions of who has the right to call themselves or others creative, or to deem certain endeavors as not worthwhile. However, the fact remains that millions of crafters encounter art education through popular craft pedagogy.

Popular Craft and Art Education

While traditional crafting has a long history across cultures (Barber, 1994; Metcalf, 1993), popular or mass craft is a relatively new phenomena. The concept of a prepackaged kit that contains everything needed to assemble an inexpensive finished craft object is even more recent, probably starting around the 1920s. Today, large chain stores such as Hobby Lobby and JoAnn are devoted entirely to such craft materials and kits. Some stores even feature classes and workshops (Grover, 1997; Schifrin,1998). It could be argued that from an economic and sociocultural perspective, popular craft is the most democratic of visual art forms in existence. Today's craft materials are cheap, plentiful, and offer the crafter an array of colorful, tantalizing textures. Glitter adhesives, mylar stick-on's, holographic papers and neon felt are but a few examples of a celebration of both personal decoration and consumer prowess.

In many ways, such materials are rebellious in their assertion of artificiality, considering art education's adherence to the "authentic" art experience (Lowenfeld, 1987). Even more daring are the motifs and themes common to most kit crafts. Religion, cute animals, country styles, babies, family, patriotism, and other plays on nostalgia run counter to the detached cynicism that academia prefers.

Once in a while art education admits to noticing popular craft. With the exception of some writers who approach craft from a stance of critical inquiry (Deniston, 1997; Katter, 1995; Kellman, 1996), most view it as something to be overcome or ignored. The condemnations include the following: First, people who engage in such activities are viewed as visually uneducated, and need our artistic help (Swanger, 1993). Second, such crafts are seen as a form of aesthetic subjugation (Lowenfeld, 1987). Women who voluntarily choose crafting over fine arts are considered to suffer from false consciousness (shouldn't they be smoking cigars like the big boys or painting in the style of O'Keefe)? Third, studio craft writing indicates that it's not craft that's the problem, it's **who** is doing it. When institutionalized via the museum, it is seen as perfectly fine.

In order for craft to be intellectualized, it must reject tradition, because tradition cannot possibly possess insight of any kind. Its only purpose is to exist for our criticism or for nifty appropriation into stylish yet postmodern art installations! This view is quite common in studio "craftspeak" which tries to mimic the boundaries of the fine art world. For example, quilting is appropriated for a variety of teaching purposes, primarily used to denote "community" or "collaboration." Therefore, if making a quilt is a good thing, then an artist or group of artists making a quilt must have better insight into the mind of the process, especially if they reject the tradition of hand sewing as "too laborious." While popular craft is upfront and even playful about the use of timesaving devices in craft construction, the fine art world tries to devalue these labors.

In a review of a recent quilt exhibition, Amidon, (1997) writes: "A subsequent work titled *Quilt?!* confirms the artistic gesture against the stable definition and the traditional quilt. Far from the quilting bee narrative, the work raises intellectual issues that evoke rich complex ideas and discussion" (p. 46). What is implied here is that the quilting bee is a dead source of insight. Its efficient dismissal via text indicates that only a few people have access to intellectual meaning and discussion. And in our field, for the most part, those people are called "artists" and "art educators." So it is quite obvious where popular craft fits in: it's not included. Unfortunately, by excluding such works, we are missing out on a wonderfully postmodern aesthetic activity happening before our eyes, full of subtle ironic commentary about nostalgia, politics, gender issues, and self.

What lies within the craft kit? On the one hand we have its historical narrative based in consumerism. Large discount stores and individuals such as Aleene Jackson, inventor of "Tacky Glue" and other classic craft materials, play a part in the promotion and ongoing development of mass craft kits. On the other hand, there lies at the heart of popular craft, a bold questioning of fine art's fierce loyalty to modernist concepts of originality and self-expression. These consumerist and philosophical influences have enormous implications for art education in a postmodern society.

The Craft Kit: History Via Consumerism

Aleene's Impact on the Craft Industry

The prevailing philosophy of our industry right now is that the manufacturer should do 90% of the work, letting the consumer finish it, but also letting the consumer take 100% of the credit for the project. The manufacturer does the work—you don't have to be a crafter or have talent to do crafts anymore. The projects are so simplified that literally anybody can do them. And that also makes this a more flexible industry to a much broader segment of the demographics. (Jackson, 1997, p. 292)

I was very fortunate to come across Aleene Jackson's recent autobiography titled *Aleene: A "Tacky" Lady* (1997). The title is a play on meanings, referring, of course, to her famous Tacky Glue. Yet, it also implies the risk of appearing kitsch-y or overdone when one engages in the making of popular craft items. Many assumptions are made when visual works exist on the margins of fine art.

Aleene has no apologies for seeing popular craft as a money making endeavor, nor does she disguise its directive or "how-to" nature. In 1945 she recognized the need for craft kits and, from her florist shop, she supplied hard to find items for making corsages. Part of the key to Aleene's success is found in the following cliche: being at the right place at the right time. For example, she and her father were the first people in the business to cut Styrofoam (a Dow product) into shapes for crafting (Jackson, 1997). This led to her being a spokesperson for the company and resulted in two project books for the emerging crafts industry (pp. 36-37). These are considered to be her first instructional publications.

Aleene deliberately kept her "how to" writing as simple as possible so that anyone would feel comfortable with trying a new craft technique or material (p. 41). The simplicity of such instructional text is remarkable on many levels. Art educators may find the concept of reducing an aesthetic process to its minimum components problematic, but one could argue that Discipline Based Art Education (DBAE) accomplishes this same goal, though with more advanced vocabulary. While the "how to" can be viewed as a patronizing gesture, it also makes a democratic attempt to include everyone in the process of creating an object.

For Aleene, television was a perfect avenue for communicating her instructional crafts. Even the name of her 1951 program, "Fun With Flowers" suggests an openness to the idea that making things is about pleasure. · To keep the crafters happy, Aleene's television shows led to her marketing such products as Formosan Wood Fibre (used to make flower forms), Styrofoam, and Tacky Glue. Each product had its own sheet of directions. The idea was to engage the crafter in experimentation with the same basic products, only combined in new ways.

Aleene writes: "There was no craft industry in the early 50s. What there was were individuals throughout the country who practiced crafts, some of them making and selling products and supplies, but there was virtually no 'industry' to speak of" (p. 66). Thus, the crafts we have become accustomed to seeing in church bazaars and mall shows are a relatively recent phenomena. Obviously Aleene sensed a need somewhere in the populace to create a craft industry as influential as the then male-dominated Hobby Industry Association (HIA), which was busy promoting model kits at the time. Today, the HIA is primarily comprised of craft-related businesses rather than model kit manufacturers.

For Aleene, popular craft is about constant change. Each time she and her family would take their "Craft Caravan" displays on the road, they would have something new to show at their "make it and take it" events during the '60s and '70s:

> We published a catalogue of products we were offering. I remember that at Christmas we did Tissue Paper Wreaths, Deco Foil Angels, and Chenille Bump Christmas Tree Corsages. For Easter we offered things like Feather Easter Lilies, and an assortment of ducks using Styrofoam shapes of course. I was always coming up with new products and ways to package and market ideas. (p. 126)

The "Craft Caravan" gave way to Aleene's highly popular Craft Club, which is still going strong today. Subscribers pay a small fee which gets them how-to sheets, product updates, and guest crafters' projects. Today's Craft Club coincides with Aleene's Creative Living, a one-hour television program. Whatever is featured for the month of programming will arrive in subscribers' mail boxes soon thereafter. The television show also offers "Get Acquainted Kits, "based on featured products. The viewer simply orders the entire kit of supplies needed with no outside shopping involved. Finally, there is *Aleene's Creative Living Magazine* which also displays the same craft projects.

Without a doubt, the craft kit as we know it would not exist without the work of Aleene Jackson. Larger chain stores such as Wal-Mart,

Hobby Lobby, and JoAnn have used the craft kit concept to their advantage. Combined with their ability to buy in mass quantities, large chain stores present popular craft as a force to be reckoned with.

Bigger as Better: Contemporary Craft Retailers

Aleene's autobiography mentions how early craft retailers were small, independent stores (Jackson, 1997, pp. 65-66). Today, this is not the case. Large chain stores and "supercenters" are here to stay, in towns both large and small. Supercenters are an American derivative of the European "hypermarts," usually housed in buildings containing 100,000 to 250,000 square feet. More than a discount department store, the supercenter offers groceries, portrait studios, banks, video rentals, optical services, dry cleaning, and hair salons, all under one roof (Graff, 1998).

The supercenter, like the craft kit, is a new phenomena, and Wal-Mart leads the way. Sam Walton, its founder, was instrumental in defining the unique culture of American discounting beginning in the early '60s. After a decade of operating several Ben Franklin dime stores in Arkansas, he decided to experiment with deep discounting and high volume selling. In the early days of Wal-Mart, it was not unusual to find outrageous promotional schemes such as 12-foot wide detergent pyramids, snack food eating contests and precision shopping cart drill teams (Huey &Walton,1993).

Wal-Mart's craft departments are a holdover from these early displays. Center kiosks are filled to the ceiling with silk flowers; shelves are crammed with pastel yarns. Stuffing is sold directly from shipping cartons, and those are stacked tall. Opulence is achieved by sheer volume, yet the average crafter can always afford to shop here.

Part of Wal-Mart's success can be attributed to its strategies of location. Unlike K-Mart, who builds stores in suburban locations, Wal-Mart enters rural towns, usually with the support of customers and to the disdain of smaller retailers. Its diffusion strategy includes a saturation of low population centers, working outward to metropolitan areas. By the time Wal-Mart entered the urban market, it had already built a strong manufacturing and distribution base in these small towns (Graff, 1998). With the average supercenter located in counties of fewer than 50,000 people, it is no surprise that the craft kit has managed to reach even the most remotely located crafters.

At this point it should be noted that there has been recent controversy concerning Wal-Mart's business practices, especially since Sam E. Walton's death. While issues such as the use of exploited foreign labor to produce goods, wage legislation, and threatened small merchants are indeed important to consider, for this particular chapter I am choosing to focus only on marketing strategies and product availability as it pertains to popular crafting. The topic of what goes into the manufacture of craft supplies is left to another time.

It can certainly be argued that Wal-Mart's success led other retailers such as Hobby Lobby and JoAnn to create mega-stores that filled the craft niche better than Sam Walton himself. Hobby Lobby opened in 1972 as a picture framing company based in Oklahoma City. Today, each retail center stocks over 60,000 craft products. David Green, president and founder includes this quote in the company's website: "We believe that it is by God's grace and provision that Hobby Lobby has endured" (Green, 1998). Juxtaposed with this declaration is a more fiscally minded mission statement: "Offering our customers an exceptional selection and unbeatable value" (Green, 1998). Popular craft's peculiar merging of religion with consumerism makes for a fascinating alliance, especially in the South.

JoAnn stores began in the '40s as an independent fabric shop in Cleveland. By 1960, the shop had grown to 50 stores. With increased reliance on inexpensive manufactured imports in the late '70s and early '80s, sewing and home decorating hit a slump. JoAnn decided to compete by offering a larger variety of other craft oriented products and kits. Many of these craft supplies are imported, but their affordability helped to counteract the appeal of ready made goods. In 1995, JoAnn opened a large retail store that included on-site classes and workshops. The store even provided day care services so that women could shop or take classes with greater ease. Chief Executive Alan Rosskamm says, "Our dream is to be the Home Depot for the creative woman, a soft Home Depot" (Schrifrin, 1998, p.1).

Arts and crafts materials make up an estimated 14 billion dollars in retail business, having almost doubled in the past five years. Grover (1997) argues that this surge is due in part to the impersonality of the computer age coupled with increased interest in wise use of precious leisure time (p. 2). Even with such booming business, though, craft supplies are a tough area of retailing to master. One major problem found here is slow inventory turnover. In order for stores to attract customers, they need to stock several colors of one item, such as paint or thread, and this makes for sluggish sales in these areas (Schrifrin, 1998).

Legislation such as the Consumer Goods Pricing Act of 1975 made it possible for discount retailers to stock their inventory cheaper than ever before. Prior to this legislation, manufacturers could control the resale pricing of their goods as well as the amount of important product information revealed to buyers. Since 1975, manufacturers have had to resort to other ways (besides the service-oriented small businesses of the past) to convey product information to the customer. This meant an emphasis on trademarks, elaborate display setups, and fancier packaging (Boyd, 1997). Popular craft has certainly experienced a different sort of marketing since the mid-'70s.

Conclusion: Why Originality?

In looking at kit crafts, the problem is not how to push for making craft into art, but to focus on the question: What is this activity known as popular craft? Turning the study of craft into an art vs. craft crusade is a trite approach to the subject and shows little respect for the complexity of craft and crafting today. Craft is distinct from art in many ways and should be respected for its uniqueness and connections to people (Metcalf, 1993). Too much has been written on the art/craft debate already. It's time to get beyond assertions of who's better/who's equal and look into what is special about crafts' more popular forms.

A reviewing of craft as more than just "common sense art" and recognizing it as a meaning-making endeavor also calls for rethinking our ideas of originality and how they are tied to modernism (Dissanayake, 1988; Wolff, 1981). A reliance on originality makes the artist into a metaphysical being, as if 'he' were given some sort of magical talent.

Postmodern analysis has pointed out instances of art being shaped by society, not the other way around (Wolff, 1981). Opening the dialogue of art to include group activities such as kit crafts, promotes a democratic space for debate and discussion to occur and to elicit exciting possibilities.

Kit crafts have a great deal to do with the notion of a postmodern community. This community is both social and isolating at once as crafting is marked by periods of solitude and sharing. Expression of community goes against the ideal of individuality as taught in schools and in the dominant art education curriculum. We can view the sameness of craft items as expressions of their community interests and values. Perhaps it is more important for kit crafters to adhere to the community (however transient and commercial) and create anonymous objects, than to make individualistic "original" artworks.

References

Amidon, C. (1997). "Is there still a place for fiber art?" *Fiberarts, 24*(3), 42-47.

Barber, E. (1994). *Women's work: The first 20,000 years.* New York: W. W. Norton.

Boyd, D. (1997). "From 'mom and pop' to Wal-Mart: The impact of the Consumer Goods Pricing Act of 1975 on the retail sector of the United States." *Journal of Economic Issues, 31*(1), 223-233.

Deniston, G. (1997). "Gender and age: Out of our yards, sight, and minds." *The Journal of Social Theory in Art Education, 17,* 42-48.

Dissanayake, E. (1988). *What is art for?* Seattle: University of Washington Press.

Graff, T. (1998). "The locations of Wal-Mart and K-Mart supercenters: Contrasting corporate strategies." *The Professional Geographer, 50*(1), 46-58.

Green, D. (1998) "Hobby Lobby Statement of Policy." http://hobbylobby.com/site2/corp.htm.

Grover, M. (1997). "Artsy-crafty." *Forbes, 159*(5), 74-78.

Huey, J., & Walton, S. (1993). *Sam Walton: Made in America.* NY: Bantam Books.

Jackson, A. (1997). *Aleene: A "tacky" lady.* Buellton, CA: Eneela Publications.

Katter, E. (1995). "Craft and community." *Art Education, 48*(1), 8-13.

Kellman, J. (1996). "Women's handwork: Stories of similarity and diversity." *Art Education, 49*(2), 33-39.

Lowenfeld, V. (1987). *Creative and mental growth* (7th ed.). NY: Macmillan.

Metcalf, B. (1993, Feb/Mar). "Replacing the myth of modernism." *American Craft,* 40-47.

Schrifrin, M. (1998). "Bop while you shop." *Forbes, 162*(1), 69-70.

Swanger, D. (1993). "Dumbing down art in America." *Art Education, 46*(3), 52-55.

Wolff, J. (1981). *The social production of art.* New York: New York University Press.

Verna Wulfekammer's Story

Paula L. McNeill

In this historical narrative using primary sources and oral history interviews, the life and 40-year teaching career of University of Missouri-Columbia art educator and weaver, Verna Mary Wulfekammer (1900-1994) will be explored. Wulfekammer's contribution to the history of art education occurred at the local level; consequently she represented what researchers, Georgia Collins and Renee Sandell (1984), have called a hiddenstream figure: "A notable hiddenstream woman art educator could be the retired art teacher whose contributions to art education are recognized by former colleagues and pupils who recount stories of lessons she taught, exhibits she staged, her contributions to a local art society, and her overall influence on her community" (Collins & Sandell, 1984).

In "Stories of the Important Teachers in Our Lives: An Editorial," Jerome Hausman reflected on the importance of role models for teachers:

No one among us lives alone. People and events make a difference in the shaping of self-image and personal identity. Each of us develops a concept of "self" that is ever changing, subject to dialogues and interactions as memories and predispositions, hopes and aspirations interact with an evolving reality. Our mechanisms of "memory" serve as powerful forces in the shaping of our lives. For those of us who are teachers, it is said that memories of how we have been taught serve as powerful models influencing the manner in which we teach. (Hausman, 1991, p. 4)

Mentored in the mid-'20s and early '30s by her professor and colleague, Ella Victoria Dobbs, and serving as a teacher and role model for several generations of art students, Verna Wulfekammer was responsible for developing the art education and weaving programs at the University of Missouri begun by Dobbs during the early decades of the 20th century. For four decades, from 1928 to 1968, Wulfekammer contributed to the growth of the art education and weaving programs at the university. She taught and refined coursework in artcraft, bookbinding, basketry, handwork, weaving, and supervision of student teaching, courses which formed the core of the art education teacher preparation and weaving programs at Missouri.

In a 1988 interview with me, 20 years after her retirement from teaching, Wulfekammer expressed unmistakable anger at the fact that she had been an Assistant Professor for 20 years and had only obtained the rank of Associate Professor after 40 years of service to the university and state. During this time she had received unconsciously small raises in pay so that her salary was very poor, had to watch her male colleagues be promoted over her in rank and then to work for them, and in many ways felt poorly treated as a reward for her expertise, hard work, and experience. (V. Wulfekammer, personal communication, 1988)

In 1968, on the eve of the women's movement, Wulfekammer retired from active teaching at the rank of Associate Professor. At that time, she received the honorary title, "Associate Professor of Art Retired," from the College of Arts and Science. During her long career at Missouri, Wulfekammer neither benefited by promotion to full professor, nor did she receive emerita status upon retirement.

Early Career Years, 1928-1936

According to a former student, during Wulfekammer's early career she was, for the most part, under the "watchful eye" of her mentor, Ella Victoria Dobbs, or "Miss Dobbs," as she was called. (E. Siegel, personal communication, 1995)   From an administrative point of view, Wulfekammer's career at this point emerged most clearly in a report written in 1935 by the chairman of the Department of Applied Arts, forerunner to the art education program at Missouri:

> Miss Wulfekammer was appointed instructor in this department at half time in 1928. She is now on a three-fourth time basis. Her service to the department, however, has been more than generous and she has indeed been imposed upon to the point of carrying more than a full load, although on part time appointment. Since her original appointment she has secured a Master's degree and has improved her own grasp and outlook by continuous study. She has proven her ability to handle the varied projects of this department and has especially distinguished herself in the field of art for elementary and high schools. During the years 1926-28 she taught art in the elementary schools of Independence, Missouri. During the past several years, in cooperation with Dr. Phillips of the University Elementary School, Miss Wulfekammer has been developing a research project, investigating the best method of art approach for the first grades of elementary schools. We expect valuable returns from this project. The retirement of Miss Dobbs, who has for so many years and so successfully worked in this department, is in the very near future. Miss Wulfekammer seems to promise the best leadership for this department in the future. She is even more abreast of the times (i.e., methods as they are actually in operation in the schools at the present time) than is Miss Dobbs. I, therefore, recommend and especially urge that Miss Wulfekammer be given a full time appointment at a salary of $1500. This is merely the righting of an injustice which has developed over a period of years. Miss Wulfekammer has remained faithfully at her post under the assumption that eventually a full time appointment would be hers. (Report, University Archives, C:6/14/2, Box 3, f. 55)

Finally, in 1936 in order to right the injustice which had developed over a period of years concerning the rate of Wulfekammer's career advancement, she was appointed Instructor in Applied Art, a full-time position. As is often the case with mentors and their protégeés, it wasn't until Dobbs's retirement in 1936 that Wulfekammer could begin to establish a career of her own. In some ways Wulfekammer may have unconsciously modeled her own professional life on that of Dobbs. Dobbs may have created a disciple in Wulfekammer by passing on an inheritance of her papers and artifacts to her. It is also possible that Dobbs did not want to be upstaged by her protégeé so she did not actively promote her. Before Dobbs's retirement Wulfekammer did complete some work independent of Dobbs. For example, she conducted research for her 1931 master's thesis, *The Interrelation of Free-Expression and Self-Control in the Development of Technical Skills through Creative Activities* (Wulfekammer, 1931), with C. A. Phillips in the University Elementary School, a laboratory training school modeled on John Dewey's Laboratory School of the University of Chicago.

Middle Career Years, 1936-1956

Two years after she received her master's degree in 1931, Wulfekammer took design and art appreciation courses at Teachers College, Columbia University (Dobbs's undergraduate *alma mater*), in the summer of 1933. Later that same summer she also took four units of landscape painting in Provincetown, Massachusetts, from watercolorist Charles Martin. Afterwards, sandwiched between her heavy teaching schedule, she had also managed to take classes toward her doctorate at Missouri. From 1935 to 1938, she enrolled in courses in historic ornament and art, elementary school supervision, and philosophy of education. (Western Historical Manuscript Collection, Verna M. Wulfekammer Collection, Box 1, 1938 student and teaching record)

Six years after she received her master's degree and one semester after her promotion from Instructor in Applied Art to Assistant Professor of Art, Wulfekammer discussed her application for a Doctor of Education degree in a February 10, 1938 letter to Henry E. Bent, Dean of the Graduate School:

I wish to present for consideration credits for Teachers College, Columbia University which have not been transferred to my University of Missouri record. A copy is enclosed. If these credits are acceptable I shall have them transferred. With my teaching job it is not feasible to enroll for more than a few hours each semester but I hope to have an opportunity for summer study again which might make possible a greater gain in meeting the requirements for a degree. Since the College of Fine Arts was discontinued in 1934-35 my appointment has come through the College of Arts and Science. Dean Tisdel, when making an inquiry regarding my advanced credits last year, expressed his approval and desire that I continue study toward a doctor's degree. Dr. Phillips [C. E. Phillips], whom I have consulted from time to time regarding my study program recommends that a committee make further decision regarding the requirements in my case, for a degree of Doctor of Education. (University Archives, University of Missouri, C:6/14/2, Box 3, f. 55)

Apparently from her 1938 letter to Dean Bent, Wulfekammer wanted to continue her education and attempted course work toward a doctorate in addition to teaching full-time. Furthermore, Dean Tisdel supported her ambition to obtain a doctoral degree; however, after 1944 according to her transcript, Wulfekammer no longer enrolled in courses at the university and apparently was no longer working towards a doctorate in education. (Western Historical Manuscript Collection, Verna M. Wulfekammer Collection, Box 1) There are no sources available to clarify why she did not complete the requirements for the doctoral program. It is possible that she had little time to devote to her own studies, because she was actively involved in teaching and administering the art education and weaving programs which increased in enrollment in the mid-1940s. Also, Wulfekammer's primary motivation for conducting post masters' work at Teachers College and her desire to obtain a doctorate may have been linked to job security and to career advancement rather than a desire for scholarly attainment.

Wulfekammer's life and career were appreciated by her family and supported by a wide system of women educators from Nelle Hause, her Bone Hill Elementary school teacher, to Ella Victoria Dobbs, her mentor, and to the members of Pi Lambda Theta, an education honorary society. She was not, however, without the support of some of her male colleagues, most notably Frederick Shane in his tireless efforts to secure for her an equitable salary, and ceramicist Robert Bussabarger who empathized with her plight in answering to both the Art Department and to the Education Department.

Although Dobbs had mentored Wulfekammer during the early stages of her academic career, and Dobbs was influential in helping Wulfekammer obtain her first teaching appointment at the university, after Dobbs's retirement in 1936, Wulfekammer was without a mentor in her own department even though Dobbs was alive, though ill, and living in Columbia until 1952. From Wulfekammer's biography of Dobbs, *Ella Victoria Dobbs: A Portrait Biography* (Wulfekammer, 1961), one is left with the impression that Wulfekammer's own values of loyalty and service to teaching and family were of primary importance to her and that she may have consciously modeled her professional life on that of Dobbs. In some ways, her unrelenting devotion to her mentor may have also created a hardship for her. When I first began my research on Wulfekammer she was generally known for teaching weaving and writing Dobbs's biography. On the influence of Dobbs on Wulfekammer, one of Wulfekammer's former students wrote:

Ella Victoria Dobbs was mentor and role model for Verna Wulfekammer in bringing art into the public school curriculum. In the 1920s Dobbs was an innovator; from the 30s to her retirement, Verna Wulfekammer was a dedicated 'disciple' of Dobbs, perpetuating the twenties' innovations through the next four decades. Miss Dobbs displayed independent spark, heightened by a sharp tongue and mind; Miss Wulfekammer had graciousness, gentility and almost a reverence for her mentor. This respect for her teacher reflected in Verna Wulfekammer's teaching, perhaps diminishing growth of her own stature. (N. Powell, personal communication, 1995)

Was Wulfekammer isolated by the very nature of the subject she taught in a fine arts department? She taught weaving in an era when crafts were just beginning to emerge as part of the fine arts, and she was a teacher of teachers. Important questions emerge from this: If Wulfekammer had been an artist first and a teacher second, would her career have gone differently? If her primary appointment had been in the College of Education and not in the College of Arts and Science, would it have made a difference in the rate of her career advancement? One of Wulfekammer's former students from the '40s, who later received an MFA from Cranbrook Academy of Art, commented:

> Perhaps placement of artcraft and art education classes in the department of art was inappropriate and a factor in Verna Wulfekammmer's isolation from other art faculty members. Had her teaching been a part of the College of Education, the multiple curricula she developed for the State Department of Education could have been recognized in the basic educational field. By standards of the art department, Verna Wulfekammer was not an artist; neither was work produced in her classes regarded as art. By standards of the College of Education, the projects she presented were appropriate learning skills for elementary grades in basic learning, using crafts as a means to develop motor skills, rather than to encourage creative expression. Not having to battle the frustrations of misfit, Verna Wulfekammer might have found a receptive place in the College of Education in which her services to the University were recognized more fully. (N. Powell, personal communication, 1995)

According to the same student, "The influence of Verna Wulfekammer's teaching extended into the greater community. Her emphasis upon weaving as a skill for teachers to learn quality craftsmanship was instrumental in the formation of the Columbia Weavers Guild." (N. Powell, personal communication, 1995)

Wulfekammer was not shy about demanding her rights in terms of tenure and promotion. Her publication record—necessary for tenure— was substantial, and since many things were written for state publications, these would have had some status. In 1951, after 23 years of service to the University, Wulfekammer received tenure and, in September 1956, promotion to Associate Professor at a salary of $5000. (University Archives, C:6/9/1, College of Arts and Science, Advising and Personnel Services, Faculty Personnel Files)

Late Career Years, 1956-1968

During the last 10 years of Wulfekammer's career and to his credit,

Frederick Shane, Wulfekammer's chairman and a prominent painter in the Midwest, consistently recommended her for salary increases primarily based on her service to art education. This was done even though Shane had stated in a letter to Dean William Francis English that Wulfekammer was not very creative. (University Archives, C:6/1/ 1, Box 4, f. Am-Ar) If Shane was correct in his assessment that Wulfekammer was not very creative, he nonetheless valued her teaching and service enough to recommend her for equitable raises. Apparently English differed in his assessment of Wulfekammer's value to the university since so little action was taken on his part to see that Wulfekammer received equitable salary increases.

Although Shane supported salary increases for Wulfekammer, there is no evidence that he actively worked for her promotion from Associate Professor to Full Professor when she requested a change in rank in 1961:

Professor Verna Wulfekammer has asked for a promotion to Full Professorship. She is at present earning $6200 per year. While Miss Wulfekammer is not the strongest teacher in Art Education, she does perform a valuable service in her statewide art education activities. It is possible that we might lose sight of the importance of her work in this field. To keep her at such an extremely low salary in view of her many years of service and experience cannot increase her value to the Department and the University, but on the contrary will tend to work in the opposite direction, thus I believe it would be for the best interests of the Department and the University to grant her approximately 8% or $500. (University Archives, C:6/1/1, box 4, f. Am-Ar)

If Wulfekammer had received a doctoral degree would the university have promoted her? Would she have then been in place to receive emerita status upon retiring?

Given Wulfekammer's research interests as attested by her publications: art appreciation (picture study books); curriculum (art guides for Missouri); history (Missouri Art Education Association history); and biography (*Ella Victoria Dobbs: A Portrait Biography*) would she have been better off careerwise having an academic home in the College of Education where publications were probably valued more than an exhibition record?

In 1968 Wulfekammer retired at a low salary of $9000 and was never promoted to full professor. (University Archives, C:6/1/1, box 4, f. Am-Ar) Important to her personal life, 1968 also marked the year that her elderly mother died. Wulfekammer had been taking care of her since the late '40s.

It seems reasonable to believe that, given her long-standing teaching and service to the university and to the state, she should have been promoted to full professor at some point in her 40-year career, and should have received greater remuneration for her years of dedicated service to the university. Apparently there was a recognized need to study equalization of salaries, for in 1971, three years after Wulfekammer retired, College of Arts and Science Dean, Armon F. Yanders, appointed members to the Arts and Science Committee on the Status of Women. This committee was formed to study salaries in the College of Arts and Science and to bring women's salaries up to the average male salary in the College and to later study the history of promotion and tenure in the College. (University Archives, C: 1/16/2, Box 17, f. 28)

Since Wulfekammer's superiors did not rate her teaching as very strong or creative, it is valuable to know what her former students and colleagues thought of her. In a 1995 letter Ralph Jacobs, professor of art education at Mankato State University, reminisces about Wulfekammer, his professor in the late '50s to the early '60s:

> I think of her with respect and admiration. VMW was a good teacher, and an inspiration to me. She was one of my own mentors in my early college student career, and her support of me is very much appreciated. My entire professional career has been positively influenced by this kind, nurturing and caring woman. While not particularly active or aggressive in the art education community in our country, VMW was always alert to what was going on, to research in art education, to theory and practice concerns. Her professional outlook was current. (R. Jacobs, personal communication, 1995)

Robert Bussabarger, Professor Emeritus of Art, writes that Wulfekammer was:

overshadowed by the dominant personality of V. Dobbs [Ella Victoria Dobbs], her mentor, who was from all indications a strong feminist. The age in which Verna lived was probably not conducive to women's rights and respect and affected her potential. Arts and crafts and teaching school became an acceptable place for women's occupations from the turn of the century but not particularly a place for financial gain and respect. She was never able to wield much power and influence in academic circles...yet in spite of this under-dog situation she was able to quietly affect the lives, direction, and artistic sensibilities of countless students. (R. Bussabarger, personal communication, 1995)

Important questions resurface time and time again in the field of art education: What is the ideal model of academic success for art educators in a fine arts department? Should art educators be expected to be both exhibiting artists and publishing teachers? How do women receive and make use of mentoring in professions which are over-whelmingly populated by males? Questions continue about why women receive lower level jobs and fewer promotions—because they are perceived as less qualified—or are they not so highly qualified because of outside forces which discourage them from earning PhDs, such as family commitments, fear of being "overeducated," and economic factors. To what extent is this all changing?

Wulfekammer's lifetime (1900 to 1994) spanned the history of art education from its emergence around the turn of the century from manual and applied arts to its forming a discipline-based approach to art education (DBAE) in the 1980s. During her lifetime Wulfekammer witnessed the emergence of crafts as a fine art, plus some improvement in the status of women in art faculty positions, but unfortunately, not for her.

Finally, in 1994, 26 years after her retirement from the university, Wulfekammer received a Citation of Merit for Outstanding Achievement and Meritorious Service to Education by the Alumni Association of the College of Education. Because her failing health prevented her from attending the awards ceremony, the guardian and conservator of her estate, accepted the award.

On the occasion of the awards ceremony, one of Wulfekammer's former students from the 1930s said:

Since my dad was an MU [University of Missouri] professor, 1910-1958, I have some limited knowledge about how MU operates, but I don't remember hearing any criticism or negative remarks concerning Verna. Apparently she was overlooked far too long. I was delighted when I heard the School of Education was giving her an award—which I'm sure she well deserved—and I regret the honor was delayed so long that her health didn't permit her to attend in person. By the time I saw her in the hospital, she didn't recognize me. (E. Siegel, personal communication, 1995)

Two months later, Verna Wulfekammer died at age 94. Surprisingly, when her will was probated she left a portion of her estate to the University of Missouri to establish the "Verna Wulfekammer Art Education Doctoral Fellowship" for the study of weaving and its applications. Ironically, she had created her own memorial and a legacy that will continue to live on in the careers and lives of her students.

References

Collins, G., & Sandell, R. (1984). *Women, art, and education.* Reston, VA: National Art Education Association.

Hausman, J.J. (1991). Stories of the important teachers in our lives. *Art Education, 44* (4), 4-5.

University Archives, University of Missouri-Columbia. Report, C:6/14/2, Box 3, f. 55. College of Arts and Science, Advising and Personnel Services, Faculty Personnel Files, C:6/9/1. C:6/1/1, Box 4, f. Am-Ar. C: 1/16/2, Box 17, f. 28.

Wulfekammer, Verna M. Collection. Western Historical Manuscript Collection, University of Missouri-Columbia. Box 1, 1938 student and teaching record.

Wulfekammer, V. (1931). *The interrelation of free-expression and self-control in the development of technical skills through creative activities.* Unpublished master's thesis, University of Missouri-Columbia.

Wulfekammer, V. (1961). *Ella Victoria Dobbs: A portrait biography.* Columbia, MO: Pi Lambda Theta .

10

Elizabeth Stein: My Teacher

Alice Arnold

When we reflect on the people who have influenced our lives the most, we often remember a favorite teacher, a person who cared and showed us their care in a myriad of ways. I have been fortunate in my life and have had a long list of good teachers. But one stands out as truly wonderful—my high school art teacher—Miss Elizabeth Stein.

In the summer of 1998 I drove from my home in North Carolina to her residence in Chicago, Illinois, for a visit and a return to "the windy city" of my youth. It was Sunday evening, July 12, 1998, more than 30 years since Miss Stein had been my art teacher at Bloomington High School. The following conversation captures the spirit of this remarkable teacher.

Arnold: I'd like to talk about three aspects of your career: your early life—your training and education, your days at Bloomington High School, and what you have been doing since then. I graduated thirty years ago from Bloomington High School. Tell me a little bit about your life.

Stein: I graduated from high school in 1924 and from college in 1929. I was not planning to get married, as most people were, and needed something to do, so I did volunteer work at Michael Reese Hospital in Occupational Therapy. I liked that very much. It was along the lines of art, but not quite. Anyway, then I went to a testing service where they ask a lot of questions and try to outline what you would be best suited for, and they went into all kinds of aspects of your interests and personality. They concluded that I would be suitable for either occupational therapy or teaching.

So, from that time on I guess I began to consider teaching. I did go to the Art Institute of Chicago and got a degree in Art Education and there were openings available. I first got a job in Sioux Falls, South Dakota, which was terribly remote from Chicago, but there was a group of us all coming from the Art Institute, and so we had a very nice time there all together. I stayed there for two years. We were told we must stay in our first job for two years. I wanted to move a little closer to Chicago and then I was able to get a job in Kenosha, which is not at all that far. In fact, it was too near, because then you tend to come home all the time. But it was not a particularly interesting place to stay in your spare time, so it was very easy to take the train and come home. I stayed there for two years until the fellow who was in my job, who had been in the service, came back from the service. He wanted his job back. It was very simple for me to leave.

I then looked for another job and, let's see…then I went to an agency. They had this job opening in Bloomington (Illinois). Well, Bloomington had a very good reputation at the time for its cultural background and university, so I had an opportunity to be interviewed there. I interviewed with Mr. Wells, the superintendent, and I slipped into that job. Now, what year was that…1948 or '49, I'm not sure exactly.

Arnold: That sounds about right. I had you as a teacher in 1968 and I had transferred over from another school in town.

Stein: Oh, had you?

Arnold: Yes, and I found the program very, very good at BHS. I found it very interesting.

Stein: You mean just the art program?

Arnold: Yes, I found the art program very interesting.

Stein: Oh, this was the old school too. And it was Mr. Kurtz, the principal. Remember him?

Arnold: No.

Stein: Oh, he was very dynamic. I liked him very much. He didn't know a thing about the art program, or didn't care particularly. He approved everything I did.

Arnold: Sure. Well, I found there was a lot of structure in the program, and I needed that. I felt there were high standards. It was high quality. We had sketchbooks that were due every Monday morning.

Stein: Oh, yes.

Arnold: That's how we all learned to draw so well.

Stein: And every six weeks you turned them in to get graded.

Arnold: Yes.

Stein: And you always had to draw something at home...

Arnold: Usually during the weekend...

Stein: Something at the zoo possibly.

Arnold: Sometimes we went out to the old barns . . .

Stein: ...and across the street where Mary Bell's Antique Shop was and she had all her stuff out in the yard. We used to go over there and draw.

Arnold: Yes. I remember that quite well. And I enjoyed the other things, other than drawing. I liked the enameling, the work with clay, and printmaking. We printed and made our own clothes.

Stein: I was not a particularly strong artist myself. I was very much interested in the craft line, and very much interested in the clay and all the odd things we did, like printing on cloth, and then of course, we did a lot with the history of art in the sense that I had a collection of master prints of great artists and we would have a bulletin board of those and talk about those artists. And then, of course, out of doors, always drawing from nature whenever possible.

Arnold: I think maybe that's part of what I liked about the class. It was more relaxed than my regular classes. I liked the outside. I had a certain affinity for art. It wasn't a text based subject. And I was good in art. I was encouraged by my family, and I was encouraged by you.

Stein: That helps a lot, of course. You remember as I can picture it right now that school room looking toward the windows where the trees, the high trees were always so beautiful at different times of the year. Great big trees showing up in those third floor windows.

Arnold: I was in the new school.

Stein: There we had the out of doors right at out doorstep. You could step right out. That was great to have a door that you could go out.

Arnold: It was. And very often we'd go to your house for picnics. And we'd all go over there and have our picture taken and you shared the pictures with us. Sometimes we have the clothes that we made on, and that was a fun thing. Then I entered the Scholastic Art

Awards and I won with my watercolor. I did a watercolor of a group of mushrooms.

Stein: Oh yes, I remember those.

Arnold: And I won. And I got to go to Peoria and you went with me.

Stein: Now, I should have an article that tells about that. I know I had several articles telling about the winners in competitions, and I'm surprised I haven't found one that tells about you. Maybe I'll find it when I go back.

Arnold: But that was the one time in high school that I really got a lot of recognition.

Stein: That was wonderful, and you know, I think Danny Donovan did too at one time. Different people, all kinds of different people of course, that we had that won different awards. And incidentally, since you say you were in the new school then, it was Mr. Wheeler and he was a honey. He was a great favorite of mine. He used to come by all the time. He was a musician himself and so he appreciated what was going on in the art room much more than Mr. Kurtz did. He understood.

Arnold: That support is terribly important. It makes all the difference.

Stein: Well, I got along with both of them. But Mr. Wheeler was really one of my favorites. Now there was a time this year when something in the papers suggested that as we were celebrating all the different occasions: Mother's Day, Father's Day, and everybody else's day, we should have a week when you would acknowledge to someone what an influence they've had in your life. And I wrote to Mr. Wheeler because he stood out so—as not many people did. So I got a wonderful letter back from him.

Arnold: Oh, that's great.

Stein: And I kept that letter.

Arnold: That's wonderful. Do you remember anything about me at BHS?

Stein: I don't. I have an awful time remembering people in the classroom.

Arnold: I remember coming back to art class after school. School was out at 3:30, I think, and coming back and working on my enameling, my jewelry, for hours and you were there. Sometimes there was just the two of us, or a couple of other students, but you seemed to take the time to be around, be there, as long as the students wanted to work after school.

Stein: I'm lucky that way. I had no one at home waiting for me. And I didn't have a dog that I had to feed, or a cat that I had to let out, or anybody that was waiting for supper, and so my time was my own and I really enjoyed that. I never felt any pressure and that was very nice.

Arnold: And in the summer…what did you do in the summers?

Stein: Well, I had many opportunities for travel in the summer. Usually I'd be gone for, well, we used to spend quite a lot of time on trips in those days, not like now where you do two or three weeks. We went for five or six weeks anyway. I was very fortunate if I had some nice friend to go with me to Europe or we traveled extensively in the West and saw all of the wonders of the United States in the West. We went to Alaska. Actually I went to Alaska by myself one time. That's the only trip I took by myself.

Arnold: That's a place I'd like to go.

Stein: All of California and the west coast, and the Grand Canyon, Bryce Canyon, and so on.

Arnold: One thing I think is very interesting is that you have stayed in touch with so many students over the years. We said it's been thirty years for me and we've been friends for thirty years. But you have maintained friendships with many, many students and I think that's extraordinary.

Stein: I think it is too from what I know about most teachers. As it turns out, I've kept up with so many of them who've stayed in the art field and are teaching, so it always seems as though we have quite a bit in common when we get together. And often they come back to Bloomington and so I've been able to see them there. Or if they happen to come to Chicago, I see them here. I consider—strange as it may seem—I consider my ex-students my family more than my real family because I see them just as much or more. I share more with them. And, of course the family all has their own problems and their own families and keep very busy, so I enjoy especially the kids that come back that I see.

Arnold: I remember one summer you had a reunion of all your students. I don't remember what year that was...'83 or '84.

Stein: Do you remember we had an exhibit at the Library, didn't we? It was Mel Theobald who organized that, I think. I have the brochure from it.

Arnold: Yes...yes...and I was in that exhibition, I believe. And then we had a dinner or reception...

Stein: ...on Front Street.

Arnold: Yes...and that was nice

Stein: Oh, that was swell.

Arnold: I think that helped me get reacquainted at that time, actually. You had one student who has become quite famous, and that's Elizabeth Murray.

Stein: Yes, and if you ask me what she did in high school, I haven't the vaguest idea. I don't remember her work at all. I don't remember her sketchbook, which seems very odd. And I have one piece of her work that she sent me when she was in college, that's all. She has done enormously well. She's one of the outstanding women artists in the country and her work is hanging in most of the big museums. She's traveled a lot showing her work. She has a very nice family...lives in New York, and she comes here very often to speak at the Art Institute and to give master classes at the Art Institute, where she went to school. She did go there because I was able to "shove her in" and I didn't get too many kids to go to the Art Institute. Maybe the first one was Wanda Rust, who's now Wanda Dill, from St. Louis. She was the first one, I think. One of my very first students and she went to the Art Institute. Then there was Don Brown, whom I've lost altogether. He never finished. He was there at the same time as Elizabeth Murray, but didn't finish. There's just one or two others that have gone there, but Murray is tops. And everybody has the greatest respect for her. It's just wonderful to hear the comments they make about her.

Arnold: Are there any other students that you remember or that you've kept in touch with?

Stein: Well, of course, all the ones that are teachers...Lou Cabeen in Seattle, Susie Kohler in Florida, Alice Arnold in some place or other, Roger Gottschalk in Wisconsin, who else do I have... Phyllis Arnold in Houston, Mary Ellen Ponsworth in a suburb of Chicago, and Patty Mera of Indiana. That's about it.

Arnold: Have you seen things change in teaching a lot since you first started? Have you seen the challenges of teaching change quite a bit?

Stein: Well, I have no contacts. I only read about it in the paper and of course, I see the changes from that—plenty of them.

Arnold: Well, there must have been a lot. What have you been doing for the last thirty years since you left?

Stein: Well, I was just going to say teaching must have been much more pleasant in those days because we didn't have to worry about anything special at all. Just doing the job.

Arnold: I think that's right. I remember a very organized and calm classroom.

Stein: Yes, certainly. There was one big row one time and Mr. Wheeler was challenged because he wasn't the kind of guy to settle a fight. And he didn't. And I think Mr. Bryant came along...who was a great big guy, teacher, and he was able to settle that fight...

Arnold: Oh, my!

Stein: ...and he became the principal. Mr. Wheeler took a job at another school.

Arnold: That's interesting. It's changed a lot since 1968. Now tell me a little bit about what you've been doing since you retired. You've been doing so many things. I get photographs, or postcards, from you all the time.

Stein: Well, I started out trying to find spots that would show some of my work. The first spot I found was very lucky. It was at the School of the Art Institute in Chicago. They had a small show and I was showing only color photography which wasn't so old at that time. I don't know when it was introduced. I should research that. And then I went to Springfield, to the museum there, with a very nice fellow named Bob Evans, who took my show. It was the first show of photography that that museum had had. Then later I had another show in Springfield. In the meantime, I took myself over to Peoria and was able to get a show at Lakewood Center there. So nobody came after me. They didn't know me from Adam.

I was lucky to have a little connection at Illinois State in Bloomington, and the gallery there gave me shows. Also the Art Center gave me shows, so all the way around I got quite a few. Almost every year, or every other year, I would be able to have a show. So that kept me going on the subject of photography more and more. I got interested in all kinds of different subjects. There was nothing that didn't interest me if it was something visual.

Arnold: I remember one very, very interesting show of an abandoned building that had pigments all over the floors.

Stein: Well, I'll tell you about that because that was sort of the beginning of my second life...my life of adventure. In 1989 about, I got wind of this building. Someone took me there. It was the Cuneo press, which was a very famous operation at that time. They printed fine manuscripts, Audubon prints, Bibles, all kinds of fine things, and it was a big building on 22nd Street. They had two buildings I think it was, and one building was open to anybody who wanted to walk in. It's hard to describe the scene. It had a lot of red pigments scattered all around. It had a lot of mysterious doorways to go into and you never knew what you'd find. It had some homeless people living in it. It had racks of yarns and cloth lying around on the floor. All things that were colorful and in some way interesting to photograph. And so I just kept going, usually going there oh maybe once a week as often as I could and I had to have somebody go with me. I didn't dare go by myself because I could fall and break my neck very easily and you could open a door and you'd never know what you were going to find. And you had to open the door. And the pigment was brilliant red mostly...a lot of yellow...there were some burned out places impossible to describe. So I had a field day there and have been able to exhibit those pictures a great deal. I got very well acquainted with two of the homeless people, a man and a woman...got very much interested in them and stayed friendly with them for a long time. And finally the whole building was imploded and is no longer there, at all. But I have the records and am told that I should go to the historical society and submit them there...they might be quite interested. I haven't taken the trouble to do that. The historical society is half a mile away and sometime I hope to do it.

Arnold: It sounds like a good idea.

Stein: It's a possibility, but if they'd come here it'd be better.

Arnold: But as a series I think that was a very productive time.

Stein: The subject matter that was there was a dismembered mannequin's head lying in the red pigment on the floor.

Arnold: The postcard had a mannequin…the postcard that you sent…

Stein: The bust of a figure…the lower body part, two legs, and my friend standing holding one leg. There's an arm, and there's a foot, and these are all lying around.

Arnold: It must have been a very mysterious place.

Stein: Oh, it was. See, I have a paper written on the subject, and this lady who's putting on my next show took all my papers and all the things I've written, and put them together into one piece which is what she's written.

Arnold: And about how old were you when you were doing this?

Stein: I was in my eighties . . .

Arnold: Your eighties…and how old are you now?

Stein: In my nineties. You see, I was able to walk around. I was able bodied at this time; and the next show too when I was going to the Oscar Mayer building, I was able to crawl around everywhere without any trouble, with nobody ever with me. And I could just get what I wanted and never had a fall or anything. So those two places, that was very unusual. Then, as far as the junkyard goes, there we would only go by car and take a lot of pictures through the window. It was sort of hazardous walking around and you could only go on Sunday because there were too many dangerous things going on during the week. And they were bringing the junk in all the time, all the time, truck after truck after truck. They would weigh it and then they would take it up on the conveyer belt to be ground up metal. They said everything could be recycled. It's all ground up. And then you would see mountains of things like refrigerators and stoves all ready to be junked.

Arnold: A place that's very interesting visually.

Stein: Well, the machinery, yes. Of course, I have it all piled up over there in the other room. The pictures are ready to go. And they still fascinate me, the pieces that I photographed.

Arnold: I think that the situation of staying in touch with all these students and being so active in your own art has kept you alive and in touch with your family, your students who are your family, and has kept you young.

Stein: Well, it's kept me thinking. The visual thing is everything and what I enjoy so much is when somebody tells me, as they often do, that they never noticed these things before and now they notice them. I think that really means a lot. It happens all the time and it means a lot. It can be a color that they never noticed.

Arnold: Well, I remember when we were at Bloomington High School. You would be back from a trip, maybe to one of these beautiful islands, or to Europe. You'd bring in some shells or some things that you'd found and you'd show us the curvature of the shell and the soft pink as it moved into the beige, or as it moved into the brown...

Stein: (laughter)

Arnold: I guess I was learning to look and learning to see the beauty in the subtlety of the shell. And so I think I held onto that for all of my life. To look for the beauty and to find it in simple things...a pretty pebble, or pretty shell.

Stein: I'm also really hooked on pattern and design. On the shells you'll find these marvelous, marvelous patterns and of course, as far as color, you go to butterflies and you get wonderful patterns of color. We now have a butterfly house here in Chicago in the Field Museum where you can walk inside and the butterflies are flying around.

Arnold: Oh, how wonderful!

Stein: You should go.

Arnold: Oh, I might go to the butterfly house tomorrow.

Stein: ...at the Field Museum.

Arnold: There's just so much to do up here.

Stein: Right.

Arnold: Anything else you'd like to remember about your teaching?

Stein: I think the field trips, the encouragement to go to the zoo and get acquainted with the animals and to look at nature was very important, and to keep close to the history of art. I don't know anything more than that. That gives you just about everything.

Arnold: Thanks for your time tonight.

Stein: It was fun.

Reflection

The years from 1965 through 1968 were full of wonder and new accomplishments for me. I was a wanderer in those days, only interested in the events of "today." I had little structure in my life and rarely planned my activities. Yet, the art room was a place that made me feel secure. I enjoyed the work I did there and took pride in the completion of each project. I could see my skills develop and felt like I "fit in." It was a place where I could be successful.

Only now, 30 years later, do I realize that it was a life of dedication by my high school art teacher, Miss Stein, that created the atmosphere of caring and high standards that I thrived on. I am still learning today about this incredible woman who **chose** teaching as her profession. She chose to share her sense of joy and wonder with all of her students, and we thank her.

It seems that the "early teachers" are the most influential, the most important. Those early years are when basic values are formed and crucial decisions about identity take shape. In high school, each year is full of first experiences with layers of new meaning. Learning to drive a car, becoming skilled at the potter's wheel, learning to navigate the Internet, or take part in a school play. It's a time to discover what we are "good at," and what we might become. Good teachers are an essential component of this time of self-discovery. They have the capacity and impact to guide the rest of our lives.

Remembering the Aesthetic Education Program: 1966 to 1976

Stanley S. Madeja

Preface

This account is not an attempt to reconstruct the history of the Aesthetic Education Program in its entirety. Rather, it is a personal view of the program from the perspective of directing its second phase from 1969 to 1976. Further, it is an attempt to document the prominent role various art educators played in its development. A more complete history of the development of the program resides in archive at the University of Illinois[1].

Background

The Aesthetic Education Program had its origins in The Penn State Seminar of 1965, from which a proposal for a research and development center for art education authored by Manuel Barkan, Jerome Hausman, and David Ecker, was submitted by The Ohio State University. This proposal was, however, rejected by the U.S. Office of Education (USOE) but the group was encouraged to resubmit a proposal for this center. A planning meeting was held in New York at the Whitney Museum, which resulted in a discussion to resubmit the project as an arts and aesthetics curriculum development program. A planning grant was awarded to Manuel Barkan for the development of a second proposal that encompassed all of the Arts. The proposal was received in 1967 by Harlan Hoffa, then art specialist for the USOE and designated program officer for the project which became The Aesthetic Education Program (AEP). The Director of the Arts and Humanities Program, which was the granting agency within the USOE, was a very influential women, Kathryn Bloom. Charles Mark, then the Deputy Director of the National Endowment for the Arts described her as "the most important woman in the arts education at that time" (Madeja, 1992, p. 3). The Aesthetic Education Program was funded as a comprehensive curriculum development project later in 1967, and it became the largest single investment of monies by the federal government for curriculum development in the arts.

Who were the people who originated the program and what was their motivation and vision at that time for arts education in our schools? The two most important individuals at the federal level were Kathryn Bloom and Harlan Hoffa. Hoffa was a strong organizing force behind the Penn State conference, two of its purposes being to educate the field about the availability of federal support for research and development in the visual arts, and to initiate the writing of proposals in order to receive federal monies for the development of art education programs. He became the advocate for the AEP program within the federal bureaucracy. In an important step, Hoffa convinced Kathryn Bloom to support the idea and through her efforts a consortium funding approach for the program was developed which included the Division of Laboratories and the Arts and Humanities Program within the USOE, plus The Ohio State University. The direction of the program was moved from one centered in the visual arts to a comprehensive arts curriculum targeted for the public schools, which could be considered basal education in the arts and aesthetics for every student. The target audience was not only art specialists within public schools, but also other teachers in related fields of study, including elementary classroom teachers. The project was divided into two phases. The first was a research and conceptual phase that reviewed the literature in curriculum research and development in each of the arts and related fields of study. From this, a set of guidelines for curriculum development in aesthetic education was written. Phase II of the program contained the curriculum development effort which used the guidelines as a theoretical and conceptual base and developed a curriculum model for grades K through 6, with supporting multimedia units of instruction.

Phase I Activities

Although the Aesthetic Education Program was centered in all the arts, its conceptual roots and stimuli resided within the visual arts under the leadership of Manuel Barkan with the assistance of David Ecker, Laura Chapman, and Jerome Hausman. Phase I lasted approximately 2 1/2 years during 1967 to 1969. Work on the project was conducted at two sites: The Ohio State University (OSU), in Columbus, and the Central Midwestern Regional Educational Laboratory (CERMEL), in St. Louis. Within that time period Laura Chapman became a key figure in the development of the guidelines for curriculum development in aesthetic education. In addition, a graduate assistant at the time, Evan J. Kern, who eventually became a co-author of the final document, was added to the staff working at OSU.

The conceptualization of a project that had its origins in more than one discipline was not an easy task, as people in the arts did not have a great deal of experience in working together on a public school curriculum. There were no existing models to assist in curriculum design, especially when the overriding focus of the program became aesthetics. However, it was clear from the beginning that this scholarly and creative effort would have its foundations in Jerome Bruner's curriculum model, operationalized by CEMREL. The model emphasized the importance of concentrating on the definition of content in the disciplines of art, music, dance, theater, and literature as a primary prerequisite for curriculum development. A working conference in the summer of 1968 was held in Aspen, Colorado, attended by the arts discipline specialists plus the working group from OSU and the laboratory staff. The purpose of the 2-week writing conference was to finalize the content of the guidelines for the curriculum development activities projected for Phase II of the project. In 1969, Ecker and Hausman decided to withdraw from the project because of their move to New York University, thus Chapman and Barkan became the guiding conceptual team. Phase I of the project concluded with the publication of the *Guidelines for Curriculum Development In Aesthetic Education* (Barkan, Chapman, & Kern, 1970).

As an extension of Phase I, the laboratory under the direction of Wade Robinson, in conjunction with the U.S. Office of Education Arts and Humanities group under the direction of Kathryn Bloom, conducted a national search for a director of Phase II. I was hired as the director and Manuel Barkan and Laura Chapman were to be the transition team as major content consultants. (Neither Barkan nor Chapman was willing to make a full-time commitment to the project, which was anticipated to last another 5 to 6 years.) It is also important to note that Kathryn Bloom left her government post and was working full time for John D. Rockefeller III, as Director of Arts in Education Program for the JDR III Fund, and I had filled Harlan Hoffa's position as Visual Arts Specialist in Art and Humanities Program and reported to Kathryn Bloom. During that time period I made occasional trips to New York to meet with Kathryn Bloom for planning what was to be the Arts in Education Program. Two of these meetings were with John D. Rockefeller III, on who's initiative the arts in education division of the JDR III Fund was being created. My involvement with the Fund at this time was the start of a continuing working relationship with their activities until their termination because of Rockefeller's death.

My first formal contact with the Aesthetic Education Program was the Aspen writing conference in the summer of 1968. During my first 3 years at the laboratory, my position was Director of the project in the University City Schools, supported by the JDR III Fund and Phase II of the CEMREL Aesthetic Education Program. I had worked closely in the last year of Phase I with the staff at OSU and primarily with Barkan, as Director of the project. This was a critical time for the program as we were making the transition from a project staff composed mainly of consultants who were nationally recognized scholars in the arts, to a full-time staff based in St. Louis. This necessitated the establishing of some bridges between the first and second phases of the project. The program plan constructed these links by retaining the 20-member advisory committee and the content consultants who worked on Phase I. In addition, Manuel Barkan and Laura Chapman were to remain as consultants to the project. Unfortunately, the best laid plans of any project are subject to human fragility, and the Aesthetic Education Program was no exception. During 1968, Manuel Barkan was diagnosed as having cancer and his health deteriorated significantly during the transition year. It was also announced by Laura Chapman in 1969, that she had decided to pursue other interests besides being a college professor at The Ohio State University and declined the invitation to become a major consultant to Phase II of the program. However, it should be noted that she was gracious and willing to consult on an informal basis throughout the years of the project. Manuel Barkan was to continue as a consultant and also act as the Visual Arts Content Specialist. However, his death left the program with a gigantic void. The task of directing the project fell upon my shoulders, as it was necessary for me to pull together the new staff members. Manuel Barkan was replaced by Reid Hastie, from the University of Minnesota, another art educator and Past President of NAEA.

Phase II Activities

The major task for Phase II of the project was to develop an aesthetic education curriculum for elementary school, grades K through 6. The goals of the program were defined as follows:

1. To construct a curriculum model based on the guidelines developed in Phase I.
2. To design and test multimedia curriculum units which act as building blocks for the curriculum and could be arranged by a school in different sequences.
3. To disseminate the curriculum model and the instructional materials to the schools.

To meet these goals, the Aesthetic Education Curriculum organized its content around 6 major areas: Aesthetics in the Physical World, Aesthetics and Arts Elements, Aesthetics and the Creative Process, Aesthetic and the Artist, Aesthetic and the Culture, Aesthetics and the Environment. Content outlines, outcomes, and concepts were defined for each center of attention, which defined the content to be taught. Forty-seven multimedia instructional units were developed and a publication program was initiated with the Lincoln Center for the Performing Arts and Viking Press in New York.

The need for the program at that time centered around the following assumptions. If aesthetic education were to be accepted in the general education program, justifications and a rationale would have to be articulated to all the populations concerned. In addition, instructional resources were needed for the arts specialists and classroom teachers who would teach aesthetic education. Instructional materials, similar to those that already existed in science, mathematics, and language arts, had to be developed in order to assist in curriculum implementation.

Aesthetic Education was not thought of as a discipline, as is art or music. Instead, it was considered in a broader context as an area of study that encompasses all the arts. Aesthetic education surrounds the full range of aesthetic phenomena. These phenomena include the aesthetic experience itself, the process by which we produce an aesthetic product, the art object or event, and the historical and cultural tradition that dictates aesthetic values. As an area of study, the content of an aesthetic education program would be organized more thematically, with broader concepts and topics using the various arts disciplines as examples rather than approaching them chronologically or historically. It was agreed that curriculum design for aesthetic education should be concerned with the introduction of aesthetic values into instruction and the development of aesthetic perception and aesthetic ways of knowing. The aesthetic experience was to be valued intrinsically (valued for itself), and the ability to perceive the form and content of the experience became characteristic of aesthetic perceptions. The arts were treated as carriers of aesthetic content and the most appropriate exemplars to study and experience. Finally, it was assumed that aesthetic education concern itself with the aesthetic qualities existing in all phenomena, and it would help the student identify, describe, analyze, interpret, judge, and value these qualities through the development of a critical language which uses not only verbalization but all the sense modalities for expression and communication. Phase II concluded with the publication of *Through the Arts to the Aesthetic* (Madeja & Onuska, 1977).

Key Participants in the Aesthetic Education Program

The Aesthetic Education Program content base consisted of art, music, dance, theater, and literature. It should be noted, however, that the motivation for and direction of the program resided within key people in art education, first and foremost Kathryn Bloom. Her background resided in the visual arts and community-based art education. In the early '40s, Kathryn Bloom was an art teacher in the Owatonna, Minnesota public schools and she participated in parts of the Owatonna Project, even though it had formally ended years before. The Owatonna project was located at the University of Minnesota, under the direction of Dean Melvin Haggarty.[2] Through this experience, she was well aware of the importance of the visual arts being connected through the schools to the community. My memories of Kathryn Bloom were collated in a symposium I organized in 1991 after her death. What follows are excerpts from the proceedings of that event.[3]

Kathryn Bloom's approach to art education was somewhat simplistic but very effective in terms of explaining itself to various constituencies. That is, she was concerned that all the arts be made available to every student in our educational systems. This implied that the arts should become a part of the design of liberal arts programs in our elementary and secondary schools, as well as in colleges and universities. Kathryn Bloom, through the various programs that she directed, tried to address this larger issue of bringing the arts into the mainstream of American public education at various levels, paralleling what the Kennedy and later Johnson administrations were advocating for the Arts in general. Some of the programs were misunderstood as they were tied to the misconception that they were projects to bring the arts into an interdisciplinary configuration which in some way impinged on the integrity of the disciplines in each of the arts. This was not the case; in fact, just the opposite was true. What Kathryn Bloom was attempting to do was to support the disciplines in each of the arts and broaden their impact or base within the general education curriculum so that they reached more than just the talented or interested students in the arts. She accepted two general goals for arts education in our schools: to provide pre-professional education for those students who were interested or have the requisite skills and talent to pursue the arts as a professional activity, and to provide a liberal education in the arts for every student in the school with the same kind of commitment and resources allocated to the sciences, language arts, and/or social sciences. Kathryn Bloom's contributions to art education were that she helped to make the public aware of primary issues in the field and introduced art education to school administrators, corporate leaders, government officials, and educational leaders who had never thought deeply about issues in this field. She was one of the first in our field to recognize the importance of state departments of education and the essential need to strengthen the presence of the arts in those agencies. Also, she saw the necessity of working with the body politic of schools, the school boards, and administrators, in order to improve their perceptions of the arts as a major part of general education.

Another major contribution was Kathryn Bloom's position that the arts were stronger when bound together in our schools than they were as separate entities. This did not mean she advocated that the arts should be engaged in a forced synthesis of subject matter. She believed that the arts, as an area of study, had a much more powerful conceptual and argumentative position within the schools than any one of the singular arts disciplines. This meant that the arts would agree upon a general education curriculum that could be introduced into the elementary schools and be considered basic for every student in the schools, a position similar to a general science program at the elementary level. She understood that the arts disciplines were significantly different from one another, and at the appropriate time, specialized instruction in art, music, dance, or theater was necessary within educational programs and should emerge in the public school curriculum.

A far-reaching contribution of her years with the U.S. Office of education and the JDR III Fund was her impact on state departments of education. Through a number of the projects under her direction, such as the Aesthetic Education Program and the JDR III Fund projects, she inserted into the language of the state departments of education that the arts should be a part of general education, and she coined the phrase "Comprehensive Arts Program." The results of the effort have been manifested in many of the state guides and curriculum documents that now exist in the state departments of education—documents that either mandate or recommend that the arts exist as an integral part of general education programs. This was probably the most significant contribution she made to reach the goal of educating every student in and about the arts. It is disconcerting that Kathryn Bloom is not mentioned in most histories of art education.[4]

As mentioned earlier, Harlan Hoffa was another major participant in the Aesthetic Education Program. He worked for Kathryn Bloom as an advocate for art education at the federal level and as the visual art specialist in the Arts and Humanities Program. After leaving government service he chaired the Department of Art Education at both The Pennsylvania State University and the University of Indiana. Later he became Associate Dean of the College of Fine Arts and Architecture at Penn State. He also was President of the National Art Education Association. His influence on both of these projects cannot be understated, as he was the driving force to mold the aesthetic education project idea and acted in the advisory capacity to the program for its entirely. Harlan Hoffa had a "sixth sense" about the AEP project and what impact it might make on art education. He speculated many times that the conceptual work and theoretical constructs which the program developed probably would have a more lasting effect on the field than the program's educational materials, as they were, by their very nature, temporal. He was correct in his prediction that many of the antecedents of our present concepts of curriculum in art education resided within the Aesthetic Education Program, such as the application of Bruner's curriculum design to the arts. He also foresaw the emphasis on defining the content of each discipline before going forward with the curriculum design, and the applicability of aesthetics to the art program in the form of large concepts and themes which provide organizing elements for the art curriculum.

Other key players who were art educators in the Aesthetic Education Program were Suzanne Dudley Hoffa, who acted as my assistant and then directed a statewide program in aesthetic education with the state department of education in Pennsylvania. Donald Jack Davis, now Dean of Visual Arts at North Texas University, was the first Associate Director. He pioneered the design of the now popular methods of classroom observations as an assessment strategy for the arts. He also coordinated the evaluation team of the University City Project. Jack Davis and Laura Chapman have continued to work in curriculum design and implementation and make outstanding contributions to the field through their publications and research and development efforts. Nadine Meyers Saitlin was another Associate Director, and played a major role in the conceptualization of the curriculum model and the management of the educational materials development group. She is now executive director of the Illinois Alliance for Arts Education. Saitlin has taken a national leadership role in the development of state arts education goals and in the statewide arts assessment programs.

The era of large scale curriculum projects has passed. The ideas in establishing and carrying out The Aesthetic Education Program and the body of research remain. They are important for us to remember and build upon to further art education in our schools and in our communities.

Endnotes

[1]The archive is listed as The Aesthetic Education Archive, University of Illinois Library, Champaign/Urbana, IL.
[2]For a summary of the project see Saunders, R.J. (1985). Owatonna: Art Education's Camelot. In Hoffa, H. & Wilson, B. (Eds.). *The History of Art Education: Proceedings from the Penn State Conference*, 152-157. University Park, PA: College of Arts and Architecture, School of Visual Arts.
[3]Madeja, S.S., (Ed.). (1992b). *Kathryn Bloom, Innovation in Arts Education.* DeKalb, IL: Northern Illinois University, Art Museum, 3-12, 88-105.
[4]Kathryn Bloom's views are stated in the following article: Bloom, K. (1977). "Research and Development Needs for Comprehensive Programs in Arts in Education at the Pre-collegiate Level." In Madeja, S.S. (Ed.), *Arts and Aesthetics: An Agenda for the Future*, 317-30. St. Louis: CEMREL, Inc.

References

Barkan, M., Chapman, L.H., & Kern, E.J. (1970). *Guidelines: For curriculum development in aesthetic education.* St. Louis: CEMREL, Inc.
Madeja, S.S. (Ed.). (1992). *Kathryn Bloom, Innovations in Arts Education.* DeKalb, IL: Northern Illinois University, Art Museum.
Madeja, S.S. & Onuska, S. (1977). *Through the arts to the aesthetic.* St. Louis: CEMREL, Inc.

Community as Ethnic and Family Identification

Often when people think about community or group identification, their first response is to attend to their ethnic identity or family. Educational learning that takes place in these contexts embraces aesthetic dimensions and values related to these specific communities.

Milda Richardson writes about Elzbieta Ribokas, a Lithuanian-American who was dislocated from her homeland by war. As a way of keeping her history alive, she wove traditional sashes that communicate a way of life she felt was important to remember. June Finnegan, relating to her own Norwegian heritage, discovers how Sloyd traditions have influenced her family and the art education she values. Charles Garoian reflects on the education he had from his parents, Armenian emigrants. His teaching and performance art are clearly related to his childhood family and ethnic experiences. The art of the Guerrero Family is described by Mary Stokrocki. As with the Garoian chapter, Stokrocki demonstrates how family artistic practices and ritual, rooted in ethnic traditions, can spill over into broader communities. It would be hard to find a more influential example of family and ethnic identification extending into the broader field of art education than the work of Pedro DeLemos, editor of *The School Arts Magazine* from 1919 to 1950. DeLemos embraced his Spanish heritage in ways that captured the imagination of art teachers all over the United States. John Howell White ends this section and the anthology with his chapter illustrating how rootedness to one's individual heritage can affect an entire field of study.

Kristin G. Congdon
Co-Editor

chapter

13

Elzbieta Ribokas: Lithuanian-American Weaver and Teacher

Milda Baksys Richardson

The dislocation caused by war and political upheaval typically sends refugees into exile, leaving behind their homes and possessions. For most this exile becomes a tragedy which not even time can heal as they exhaust precious years and energy as outcasts in a frustrating attempt to retrieve lost hopes. But in any Diaspora there is always a small cadre of special people whose inner strength and insights allow them to transcend their immediate fate and to persevere in creating a new life out of the old. Instead of the physical artifacts from a former life, these idealists carry with themselves more portable and permanent instruments of realistic optimism: memories, education, and artistic impulses. By keeping open the doors of memory, a small number of exiles recapture the enchantment, the depth, and the spiritual beauty of the lost world through the invocation of history and the creation of art. One such person who brought the regenerative power of these gifts with her into exile was Elzbieta Ribokas (1905-98).[1]

A few years before Ribokas was disabled by blindness, she wove a sash — a "juosta" — to be draped across her casket, a traditional ritual associated with a Lithuanian Catholic funeral. The primary pattern is a row of white stars on a blue background along the length of the 5-inch-wide sash. The imagery evokes a place of celestial afterlife. A simple expression of faith, "Viespatie, teesie Tavo valia" ["Lord, Thy will be done"], is inscribed in the center. The small geometric patterns along the edges contain green to symbolize the fields of Ribokas's beloved Lithuanian homeland, while red stands for the flowers she loved so much. Although black was not used in traditional Lithuanian weaving because of its connotation with death, it began to appear in sashes following the Soviet occupation of Lithuania during World War II. Ribokas laid just a few black threads next to gold in the border to remind mourners of the historical importance and prosperity of Lithuania because of its strategic geographical location along the Baltic trade routes from East to West. A deeply religious woman, she prayed that she had brought some good to the world, had harmed no one, and had been made worthy of God's eternal grace.

For Ribokas[2] each sash encapsulated a voyage through life filled with hardship and tragedy, as well as fulfillment and immense joy, as symbolized by the dual forces of Yin and Yang. Just as the individual threads intertwine into patterned fabric, so the events of our lives overlap and intersect to create a holistic whole, the strength and power of which is greater than any single element or thread. For Ribokas weaving was a metaphor for the life process itself, never-ending, with infinite variety, and as each stage finishes, another is created to take its place.

Ribokas always remembered the precise moment when a casual encounter with a peasant weaver was to become the genesis of her creative life. While playing on the family estate in the Utena region of the Lithuanian Highlands, 8-year-old Ribokas saw a peasant girl weaving a narrow sash using the pick-up technique. Instead of an elaborate loom, the girl simply attached the warp threads to her waist, with the other end around a barn post. Fascination blossomed into obsession for a craft that would enrich and sustain Ribokas's life for the next 80 years.

Her early education in a local parish hall school set up in 1909 was integrated with village children, thus exposing her to traditional customs and folkways. This experience was buttressed by the growing nationalistic movements in Europe. Patriotic appreciation of historical traditions, folklife, and Lithuanian Catholicism provided the background for her growing interest in sash weaving and ethnography. In 1925, Ribokas began teaching grammar school and within a year became the principal of a school in Gelvonai (See Figure 1.), which she saved from closing. Inspired by lectures and workshops led by Antanas Tamosaitis (1906-), a renowned textile artist at the Kaunas Institute of Applied Art, she joined other intellectuals and artists during the idealistic decades of the 1920s and 1930s in collecting artifacts and recording their traditional uses (Milius, 1994). Sashes marked milestones throughout the villagers' lifetime as practical, ornamental, and ceremonial

Figure 1: Elzbieta Ribokas with her schoolchildren and parish priest in Gelvonai, 1926

objects (Tamosaitis, 1983). For everyday use, sashes served as handles for baskets, hangers for a cradle, reins for horses, and ties for flour sacks to identify the owner. From prehistoric times, the ornamental aspects were more obvious in clothing. The ceremonial and gift-giving sashes were enveloped with mysterious meaning and symbolism, playing a particularly important role in wedding customs and the cycles of agrarian life. A new bride would mark her husband's land with sashes from her dowry. She tied a sash around his plow and bound the first sheaf of the harvest with a wide sash. The mystique of the sash carried over into oral literature.

In 1934 Ribokas married Petras Ribokas, a lawyer and public prosecutor. Ribokas left teaching to manage the family farm. She exported a variety of apples from her orchards, and provided cut flowers from her large garden to the local markets. She conducted horticultural experiments with plants and berries, as well as bred cattle. As a midwife, she taught modern childcare methods to women throughout the countryside. In her personal family life she suffered the loss of her first and second born sons, both of whom died of childhood diseases. Her third child, daughter Vida, continues to be her mother's energetic agent and curator. During this period of raising a family there was little time for weaving, but the skills Ribokas learned as a community social worker, agronomist, and businesswoman would serve her well. An unexpected return to weaving arose out of the chaotic events of World War II.

As landholders, government employees, and members of the intelligentsia the Ribokas family were vulnerable to persecution by the Bolsheviks. In 1941 Ribokas was warned that her family had been targeted by authorities for deportation. That night they fled to the remote countryside and forests where they hid for several years. In 1944, they escaped to Germany and eventually arrived at the Freiburg Displaced Persons Camp in the French zone.

The Freiburg experience for the Lithuanian refugees reflects the situations vividly described by Eileen Egan (1995), in which the positive aspects of wartime are reflected in the selfless acts of individuals on behalf of those suffering. A handful of strong personalities under the dedicated leadership of the painter Vytautas K. Jonynas (1907-97), former director of the Kaunas Institute of Applied Art, created an educational environment unique in war-torn Europe (Sakalauskas, 1991; *Freiburg 1946,* 1997). At the end of World War II there were about 70,000 Lithuanian refugees in Germany, the majority of whom had been the cultural leaders in their homeland. They were clustered in various refugee camps, disoriented, disheartened, and full of fear at the news of executions and deportations by the Soviet occupiers behind the Iron Curtain. They knew they could not return home. With the help of an old friend, the French linguist Raymond Schmittlein, who was now Minister of Education in the French zone, Jonynas approached the French military government, and in 1946 received permission to establish the École des Arts et Métiers in Freiburg. The École operated until 1950 with the support of the UNRRA (United Nations Relief and Rehabilitation Agency) and BALF.[3] The school, accredited by the French and housed in renovated hotel buildings, opened with 46 students in weaving, graphics, sculpture, and ceramics. Jonynas had designed the academic program not only to nurture individual artistic expression, but also to train artists in trade skills that would be useful in adopted homelands. The emphasis

Figure 2: Sashes with geometric patterns woven by Ribokas during the Freiburg
period, 1946-49, based on 18th and 19th century artifacts. Wool pattern on
linen background

on folk art, especially weaving and ceramics, was strengthened, and
artists were encouraged to turn to folk culture for inspiration.

Antanas Tamosaitis and his wife Anastazija (1911-91), also a fiber
artist, had fled to Austria during the War and were invited by Jonynas
to head the weaving department. They arrived with their personal art
history library which was installed as a resource in the school. In
addition to weaving, the Tamosaitises organized an effective effort to
preserve traditional weaving techniques and designs by reproducing
old patterns. Ribokas became an important member of this group,
reproducing dyes and weaving sashes based on samples of older
artifacts which contained geometric patterns in wool on a linen background (See Figure 2.). Although Ribokas's primary responsibility
was at the school which had been set up for the Lithuanian children,
she collaborated with Anastazija Tamosaitis, a specialist in making
national costumes. Ribokas wove boldly colored sashes which were
coordinated with the textiles designed by her friend. Smaller sashes
were folded into diamond shapes and fashioned into elaborate head-
pieces. By the time of the last student exhibition in Freiburg, 135

students (70% of them Lithuanian) had participated in the program taught by 21 Lithuanian teachers and one Estonian. In all, the talents of about 350 refugee artists had been utilized. Many remember that the intense artistic experience in Freiburg was the one bright moment during this traumatic period of upheaval.[4] The related cultural activities—performances by dance and choir ensembles, excursions to art collections, publication of over 750 books and textbooks—not only bound the community but provided the foundation and stability from which they gathered strength for the challenges that lay ahead.[5]

After clearing customs at Ellis Island, the Ribokas family heard that Rev. Joseph Jotsevicius of St. Anthony's church in Omaha was guaranteeing jobs to immigrants who would come to his dwindling parish. Having arrived by train in Nebraska, they used the money saved from the first few years of factory work to buy a small grocery store, which Ribokas soon turned into a successful import enterprise. She also taught at the Omaha Lithuanian School which prospered as more immigrant children arrived. Following her husband's sudden death in 1964, she closed the business and moved to Brockton, Massachusetts, to live near her married daughter.

In Brockton, Ribokas's cultural activities revolved around the Lithuanian parish of St. Casimir, teaching at the Brockton Lithuanian School, and acting as correspondent for the major emigre periodicals such as *Draugas*, *Darbininkas*, and *Dirva*. But it was in her weaving that she found joy and peace to enrich her lonely widowhood. She wove 40-50 hours per week, and each year compiled a scrapbook which contained a section from each sash woven that year, with detailed notes about the occasion, pattern, thread count, and the length of time it took to weave. These albums average 60 sashes per year, varying from 3/4 of an inch in width for a doll costume, or 6 inches in length for a bookmark, to 5 inches in width and 12 feet in length for an anniversary gift. Her albums document another important aspect of the tradition in which weavers do not duplicate patterns or color combinations so that each garment or sash is unique. Prior to World War II, this was done in the spirit of friendly competition between weavers. Following the Soviet occupation, the trend shifted toward standardization of weaving, so that ensembles wearing folk costumes looked as if they were dressed in uniforms. The weaving of sashes became mechanized in factories with repetitive patterns in dull colors, in contrast to the spontaneous and colorful creations of the past. Weavers in the West insisted on maintaining the traditional priority of individuality, in part to protest the Soviet regime and to claim the continuously evolving designs as the authentic Lithuanian national expression (Saliklis, 1995). Ribokas combined elements of traditional regional patterns with boldness and invention, and incorporated seasonal colors, such as mauve or mint green, an American fashion custom unknown in Lithuania.

Figure 3: Blue cotton sash with yellow pattern of stylized ridgepole decorations.

Throughout her career she wove using the pick-up technique without a loom because she could regulate the tension of the threads with her own body. As may be seen in the blue and yellow ceremonial sash in Figure 3, she subtly wove a contrasting stripe down the center of the pattern to enliven the overall design. The red and blue zigzag along the selvedges acts as framing for the main pattern of the sash which consists of alternating diamond shapes and a more complex motif of a stylized pair of decorative ridgepole carvings found in rural architecture. In traditional Lithuanian sashes, the most common materials were flax, linen, tow, and hemp. Later wool and cotton became popular. Exotic silks in delicate shades allowed Ribokas to achieve a soft patina, and synthetic fibers such as rayon increased the range of possibilities. Most often Ribokas used boiled fast knit-cro-cheen cotton for the background and four-ply regular cotton of various thickness for the pattern. The purpose of this thread combination was to create a foundation with a glowing sheen and to raise the primary pattern from the background achieving the effect of the padded satin stitch in embroidery. Ribokas's sashes were

Figure 4: Grouping of three cotton sashes woven during the 1970s.

consistently judged to be of the highest quality because of (a) the uniqueness of the motifs, usually woven in alternating patterns—note the dramatic positioning of the deep red stylized tulips of the sash on the left in Figure 4, (b) the spacing of the motifs and intervals, (c) the complementarily of the coloration and secondary patterns in the borders, (d) the clean, crisp relationship between the face and reverse sides, and, finally, (e) the choice and combination of colors (Kudirka, 1988). A good weaver strives to achieve a rich interplay between color and rhythmic pattern in the overall design of a sash. Ribokas felt that weavers should not be restricted by inherited customs, but allow the craft to develop and adapt to modern usage (Figure 5). She was aggressive about re-creating the tradition to suit contemporary times (Hobsbawm and Ranger, 1983). Ribokas chose her palette from nature, according to her deepest feelings, or a color she associated with a particular person or holiday. Once confined to her home, she picked hues out of flower bouquets on her kitchen table or from the garden she could watch through her window. One summer, a diamond-patterned sash (Figure 6) complemented the lavender seasonal blossoms and was edged in yellow, green, and red stripes of the Lithuanian flag.

Figure 5: Sashes coordinated with contemporary upholstery fabric. The narrow
sashes will be stitched together to make decorative pillows or accent runners.

Her colleague Anastazija Tamosaitis had also been energized by
nature's moods and secrets as eloquently described by her biographer
Jonynas (1988). Upon immigration to Canada, the Tamosaitises
opened studios in Montreal and Kingston, Ontario, and became
internationally known for their work in tapestry and decorative textile
weaving. In 1977 they founded the Lithuanian Folk Art Institute with
headquarters in Kingston.[6] Branches were quickly established in
Boston, Toronto, Windsor-Detroit, Philadelphia, Chicago, and New
York. The organization's stated purpose is to collect, preserve, and
analyze ancient folk art, foster the creation of contemporary folk art,
study art of other cultures and help display and promote Lithuanian
material culture. The Canadian government supported several publications in English (Tamosaitis 1979, 1982, and 1983) and a film on
Lithuanian Textile Art. During the early years the Institute mainly
sponsored courses and workshops led by experts in the various crafts
and rewarded high-quality craftspersonship. It encouraged young
people's interest in folk art by sponsoring competitions in the émigré
Lithuanian schools. By the early 1980s the activity was redirected
toward participation in community programs and international exhibits. During the 1990s, more attention has been paid to collaborative

Figure 6: Sash showing raised diamond pattern in lavender cotton bordered by yellow, green and red stripes of the Lithuanian flag.

projects with museums, scholars, and artists in Lithuania.

Ribokas was a key member of the Boston branch established in 1978. Her sashes were frequently displayed at exhibits and cultural gatherings. In addition, Ribokas was often invited to weave ceremonial sashes as gifts for visiting dignitaries, such as Pope John Paul II in 1979. It is through the art of gift-giving that Ribokas became an informal ambassador and achieved her cultural agenda to inform the world about the political and religious plight of Lithuania during the Soviet occupation (Vardys, 1978). She and other weavers in the West changed the original function of the sashes and recontextualized their weaving to adapt it to new political and social realities in exile (Nicolaisen, 1979). For many Lithuanian priests, Ribokas wove ecclesiastical surplices where a stylized cross and wheat motifs replaced the pattern. Other variants occur when a text, such as the lyrics of the Lithuanian national anthem or a song, is woven into the gift. These presentations were not dramatic national events such as the effective protest against nuclear weapons in *The Ribbon around the Pentagon* (Pershing, 1996). Nor were the sashes examples of clandestine coding during times of oppression (Radner, 1993).[7]

Elzbieta Ribokas's life and work are polyphonic. She speaks about many human issues with authentic voices. Central to her worldview was her Catholic faith and the *communitas* it represented. As a dedicated teacher she understood the value of education not just for the privileged, but for all social classes. Education not just in an academic sense, but in an ethical sense where learned skills are engaged in meaningful work. As she taught she was never afraid to learn from people connected with autochthonous [native] culture and its traditional *ethos*. She was ever conscious of the importance of giving voice to the transcendent potential of the arts, a fact to which her legacy testifies.

Endnotes

[1] In traditional Lithuanian usage, Elzbieta's last name would appear as *Riaubaite-Ribokiene* (the daughter of Riaubas-the wife of Ribokas). The ending of a female surname indicates marriage status.
[2] My field work with Elzbieta Ribokas began in 1991 and continued until she became too weak to converse. Versions of this essay were presented at the 1992 American Folklore Society meeting in Jacksonville, Florida, and folklore seminars in Lithuania. I am deeply grateful to her daughter Vida Suziedelis for her thoughtful support throughout the project. I received gracious help from Margaret Yocom, whose insightful comments were invaluable to my research.
[3] In 1947, the UNRRA became the International Refugee Organization (IRO), one of the major components of the Marshall Plan. The acronym BALF stands for "Bendras Amerikos Lietuviu Fondas," the United Lithuanian Relief Fund of America, Inc., founded in 1944 with private funds to help Lithuanian refugees throughout the world.
[4] Artists who shared their reminiscences about the positive psychological effects of the École include Jurgis Daugvila (June 21, 1998) and Vytautas Ignas (Nov. 30, 1998).
[5] Many established successful careers in the arts (Kezys, 1994).
[6] The Board of the Lithuanian Folk Art Institute is preparing a comprehensive history. Information was generously provided by Aldona Veselka, President of the Institute, and Saulé Satas, Director of the Boston branch.
[7] Feminist theories do, however, apply to the fabrics embellished with nationalistic emblems by women during Siberian exile as a dangerously bold affirmation of ethnicity (Cepaitiené, 1994).

References

Cepaitiené, A. (1994). Tautiniai simboliai Lietuvos politiniu kaliniu ir tremtiniu rankdarbiuose [National symbols in the crafts of Lithuanian political prisoners and deportees]. *In Etnine kultura ir tautinis atgimimas [Ethnic culture and the rebirth of nationalism]* (pp. 152-160). Vilnius: Lithuanian Institute of History.

Egan, E. (1995). *For whom there is no room. Scenes from the refugee world.* Mahwah, NJ: Paulist Press.

Freiburg 1946. Art exhibit celebrating 50th anniversary of the Freiburg School of Arts and Crafts - École des Arts et Métiers (January 26 - April 3,

1997). Chicago, IL: Balzekas Museum of Lithuanian Culture,
Hobsbawm, E. & Ranger, T. (Eds.), (1983). *The invention of tradition.*
Cambridge: Cambridge University Press.

Jonynas, V.A. (1988). *Anastazija Tamosaitiene.* Kingston, Ontario:
Romuva.

Kezys, A. (1994). *Lithuanian artists in North America. Exhibitors in Daile
'91, '92, and '93.* Stickney, IL: Galerija.

Kudirka, J. (Ed.), (1988). *Spalva lietuviu liaudies mene [Color in
Lithuanian folk art].* Vilnius, Lithuania: Vaga.

Milius, V. (1994). Zemes ukio rumai—etnines kulturos puoseletojas
[Palaces of agriculture—sponsors of ethnic culture]. In *Etnine kultura ir
tautinis atgimimas [Ethnic culture and the rebirth of nationalism]* (pp. 106-
117). Vilnius: Lithuanian Institute of History.

Nicolaisen, W.F.H. (1979). Distorted function in material aspects of
culture. *Folklore Forum 12,* 223-36.

Pershing, L. (1996). *The ribbon around the Pentagon: Peace by
piecemakers.* Knoxville, TN: The University of Tennessee Press.

Radner, J.N. (Ed.), (1993). *Feminist messages. Coding in women's folk
culture.* Urbana, IL: University of Illinois Press.

Ribokiene, E. (1987, March). Lietuviu liaudes menas—juostos [Lithuanian
folk art—sashes]. *Moteru Dirva, 12.*

Sakalauskas, T. (1991). *Kelioné: Dailininko Vytauto K. Jonyno gyvenimas
[A journey: The life of painter Vytautas K. Jonynas].* Vilnius, Lithuania: Vaga.

Saliklis, R.T. (1995). *Lithuanian folk costume: A contested symbol of
national identity.* Unpublished doctoral dissertation, University of Wisconsin-
Madison.

Stasaitis, J. (1985). Elzbieta Riaubaité-Ribokiené, on the occasion of her
80th birthday. *Tremties Trimitas,* 371-372.

Tamosaitis, A. & A. (1979). *Lithuanian national costume.* Toronto, Canada:
Lithuanian Folk Art Institute.

Tamosaitis, A. (1982). *Lithuanian Easter eggs.* Toronto, Canada:
Lithuanian Folk Art Institute.

Tamosaitis, A. & A. (1983). *Lithuanian sashes.* Toronto, Canada:
Lithuanian Folk Art Institute.

Vardys, V.S. (1978). *The Catholic Church, dissent and nationality in Soviet
Lithuania.* New York: Columbia University Press.

The Influence of Scandinavian Sloyd Traditions in One American Family's Life

June Elizabeth Eyestone Finnegan

In this chapter, I examine aesthetic values in the Scandinavian-American community in which my grandmother was born and raised and how they influenced her life choices. Using a personal narrative, I place my family story in the broader context of Scandinavian domestic sloyd traditions brought to the United States and the educational sloyd movement that was prominent in Scandinavia and the United States during the late 19th and early 20th century (Eyestone, 1989, 1992). The educational sloyd movement grew out of turn-of-the-century educational reform efforts in Europe and the United States, known as manual arts training, in which the needs of the family and community were regarded as primary criteria in identifying aims and principles of the curriculum. I also examine how my grandmother's values were influential in her children's and grandchildren's life decisions, specifically my mother's and mine, and the family traditions I hope to pass on to my daughter.

My grandmother, Emma Marie Slaatta, was born on April 1, 1890, in Wilmot, South Dakota to Hellek and Ingeborg Slaathaug Slaatta. Hellek Slaatta and his first wife Gurine had immigrated to the United States from the Lunde region of Norway, which is close to Oslo, in the 1880s. After the death of Gurine, Hellek married Ingeborg. Later,

Emma[1] was born along with her twin sister, Kirsten Gurine. Ingeborg died in childbirth at the age of 19 and Kirsten died 4 months later. Annie Hegna, a teenage neighbor who lived with her parents, cared for Emma. When Annie married Gunder Vriem, 4 years later and moved to his farm, Emma accompanied them (Eyestone, 1995).

Emma's father lived in Milbank, South Dakota, where he ran a mill. Hellek was able to see his daughter only infrequently. Along with the demands of his job, transportation was limited to trains, horses, and sleigh or wagon. Emma told my mother that, although she liked horses, it was difficult to depend on them for transportation because of exposure to inclement or sub-freezing weather. Emma did not elaborate much on the earlier part of her upbringing except to express appreciation for those who raised her and the hardship of farm life in the north.

I recall a conversation with my grandmother a number of years ago in which I was expounding on my somewhat idealized and naive vision of living on a farm in olden times. I remember especially how I was comparing all the sterile packaged commodities we buy in the grocery to all the wonderful homemade things from the farm. While my grandmother agreed that farm products were good, they were a lot of work to prepare and she really appreciated being able to go the grocery store and buy everyday items so that her time was freed up to do other things. She also appreciated indoor plumbing and the cleanliness of contemporary life in how it improved the general health of everyone in the community.

No doubt due to her early life, Emma grew up as an independent person with little desire to have others do for her. The challenges of her environment created a strong sense of resourcefulness and practicality. At the time, many of those who settled in the region in which Emma lived were immigrants from Scandinavia, a number of who were from Norway. Although cultural traditions in each of the Scandinavian countries and regions varied, they had in common a strong work ethic that was related to the need to survive in a primarily cold and often harsh environment (Gaynor, 1987). Self-reliance was a necessity. This meant that if something needed to be done, you just did it. You used your best creative ability and resources to solve the challenges of daily life. For instance, if you needed a tool, you made one. This characteristic enabled many of the residents, including my grandmother, to thrive regardless of their conditions.

My grandmother's enculturation, no doubt, arose out of turn-of-the-century farming practices in Scandinavia as well as educational practices that were linked to the needs of an agrarian society (Harwood, 1898). The merging of the needs of the farm, the family, education, and the home in the peasant culture were bound by how each family member, including children, contributed to the sustenance of everyday life. This binding force was known as domestic sloyd or "hemslöjd" as it is known in Sweden (Johannesson, 1994). The products of sloyd, for instance, included tools, utensils, toys, clothing, and furniture. If something was needed, it was designed and made usually in as simple and functional a manner as possible. Occasionally, sloyd objects were decorated, generally with designs inspired by the region in which they were made, or with dates, initials, and symbols that had been handed down from generation to generation (Sterner, 1939; Thompson, 1983). One well-known sloyd object is the Dala horse, made in the province of Dalarna. The Dala horse is now considered to be a national symbol of Swedish culture. In addition to supporting family life, sloyd objects were sold or traded. Sloyd was the craft of the people.

In much of the literature on sloyd, the term is repeatedly met with difficulty with translation (Eyestone, 1989; Klein & Widbom, 1994). Early domestic sloyd included all handiwork that was created to serve the needs of survival. By examining the products of sloyd, one might decide that a "sloyder" was simply a person who made serviceable things. To teach sloyd would be to teach carpentry, metalsmithing, or other trade. However, there is agreement among early writers (i.e. Harwood, 1898; Larsson, 1893) that the true meaning of sloyd lay in the *spirit of the maker*. The result of useful and aesthetic design, skillful creation, and industrious manner, the making of sloyd objects were considered to be the embodiment of what it meant to be Scandinavian.

At the time my grandmother was beginning her life, a transitional time in Scandinavian history was evolving. As with the rest of Europe,

Russia, and the United States, industrialization was altering the fabric of society. While work and education were once the domain of the family, industrial progress was moving them into the domain of institutions, mainly factories and public schools (Eyestone, 1989). As with most changes, industrialization brought many benefits to the community as well as negative repercussions. Machine-made objects created in factories were replacing sloyd activity in the family. Those that once farmed the land were moving to factories where they worked under poor conditions. The tradition of sloyd was being lost. In response, the Swedish government passed a bill that a system for manual work be implemented in all public schools in the country (Hoffman, 1892). Although domestic sloyd could no longer be counted on for economic support to the family, it was nevertheless implemented in general education because it maintained cultural values of self-discipline, self-reliance, and aesthetic taste through handwork.

One of the most well-known systems of manual work was devised by Otto Salomon (1849-1907) in Naas, Sweden, who incorporated what was most valued about traditional sloyd while accepting the new societal changes that were taking place (Salomon, 1911). His theory for educational sloyd utilized practical, everyday skills that were employed in the home as a means for educating children to participate in a more industrialized society. Salomon headed what eventually became the Teachers' Seminarium at Naas.

In a review of the history and theory of Salomon's theory and practice of educational sloyd, Harwood (1898) noted that sloyd provided preliminary training for future artists:

> Even for the, in some ways, broader field of art there is in this training of hand and eye much that is helpful for the future. The boy or girl who has had a course in Swedish sloyd, and whose bent is for art, will be a better painter or sculptor or architect for having had such training. (p. 53)

Salomon based his theory of educational sloyd on the work of Cygnaeus (1810-1888), Pestalozzi (1746-1827), and Froebel (1782-1852). Of particular interest is the influence of Cygnaeus on Salomon's theory. Cygnaeus was the founder of public schools in

Finland and was an ardent believer in the value of handwork for general education (Hansson, 1966). He was a contemporary of Froebel and had discussed his ideas with him. Two of Cygnaeus's most characteristic aims for education were that "The occupations (or handwork) taught should be those carried on within or around the house" and that "Handwork instruction should involve the use of all tools which the Finnish peasant ordinarily possesses" (Anderson, 1926, p. 182). His attempt was to draw connections between the home and the school and to respect the traditions carried on in home life. While he did allow for the evolution of the traditions in how they might be expressed in education, he nevertheless maintained that the home-school relationship should be protected.

The teaching of educational sloyd was not limited to Scandinavia. As the theory and practice developed, sloyd schools sprang up all over Europe as well as other parts of the world where Naas graduates were willing and able to run them. In America, sloyd-training programs were started by those who were interested primarily in promoting methods of manual training. One of the most well documented promoters of educational sloyd in the United States was Gustaf Larsson. Larsson was a student of Salomon at Naas and came to America in 1888 to present the theory to get it started and then return to his native Sweden. He ended up living in Boston, however, for the rest of his life. He was responsible for founding the Sloyd Training School of Boston, later housed in the North Bennet Street Industrial School. His leadership produced many publications, speeches, and teachers trained in sloyd (Eyestone, 1989). Like Salomon before him, Larsson educated many teachers who taught sloyd all over the country as well as the world.

One of Larsson's colleagues was Lars Eriksson. Although not as influential as Larsson, Eriksson published a monthly journal called *Sloyd or Handi-work: A Manual for the Use of Schools* from 1890-1891 (Eriksson, 1891a; 1891b). In agreement with Harwood, quoted above, Eriksson also believed that through sloyd, "the child's artistic powers are developed" (Eriksson, 1891, p. 33). He elaborated by saying that "Through instruction in sloyd, the eyes of the child are trained to distinguish the beautiful from the ugly; the straight from the crooked; the clean from the dirty; the orderly from the confused." The aesthetic beliefs Eriksson held reflected traditional Scandinavian design, which overlapped beliefs held in industrial education and manual training.

As a facet of the manual training movement in the United States, educational sloyd brought the unique characteristic of the making of useful objects for the home as well as the making of completed, functional objects (Larsson, 1893). This was in contrast to other methods of manual training, such as the Russian system, that emphasized the development of skills, particularly in the area of carpentry. Ideally, this repertoire of skills would serve as a foundation for any vocation a student might purse as an adult (Larsson, 1893). However, Larsson believed along with his colleagues that the idea of creating a completed, functioning object that would be valued both in school and at home would provide motivation for a child to learn and would lead, consequently, to lifelong learning and a prosperous and healthy citizenry. The child's motivation to learn was regarded as the most critical aspect of how and why sloyd was taught. It was assumed that making a contribution to the family's sustenance and, consequently to society, was the most motivating factor for a child.

Figure 1: Emma Slaatta, graduate of South Dakota State College.

As my grandmother grew up, she was not only instilled with the values of her Scandinavian heritage, but also with her belief that a college education would provide the avenue toward independence and self-reliance. She believed strongly that being well educated was a necessary aspect of making a contribution to society. This was unusual for a young woman in the early 1900s. Even in high school, her individuality prevailed as she served as the captain of the first girls' basketball team of Wilmot High from where she was graduated in 1909 (Eyestone, 1995). The same year, she lost her father, Hellek, who was 49, to typhoid fever. She also turned 19 that year, the same age her mother was when Emma was born.

Figure 2: Cooking class, South Dakota State College.

Following graduation, Emma went to school at the Northern Normal Industrial School in Aberdeen, South Dakota, where she was graduated with a teaching certificate in 1910 (see Figure 1). She taught sixth grade for two years. Although she loved teaching, she desired a college degree and thus set out to achieve her bachelor's degree from South Dakota State College in Brookings. She accomplished her goal in 1916 with a Bachelor of Science degree in Domestic Science. Her coursework included many areas in her major including her primary interests in sewing and cooking (see Figures 2 & 3). These photographs are typical of industrial education classes, including those in the United States and Scandinavia. In the United States, scenes such as these were defined as "domestic science," whereas in Scandinavia, they might be labeled "kitchen sloyd" or "sloyd sewing" (Harwood, 1898, p. 46).

Figure 3: Sewing class, South Dakota State College.

I once asked my grandmother if her coursework included sloyd or
sloyd ideas. She replied that she didn't think so. Although she was 98
at the time, she had a relatively clear memory of her early life. I know
that, although she may not have had formal sloyd training, I believe
that prevailing values in industrial education, in relation to her upbringing and community, were influential in her education. I also
know that Emma had a lot of pride in being an American of Norwegian
descent, rather than being a Norwegian living in America. She carved
her life out of her need to survive and her desire to care for others in
the best possible way.

While a student at South Dakota State College, Emma took a course in
art appreciation. Her instructional materials included a series of prints
for her studies. She created a portfolio to protect and house the prints
of dark brown fabric. There are cardboard inserts between the outside
fabric and the inside brown paper. It is very neatly and precisely
made. The portfolio represents Emma's skill and practicality as well
as an early form of handwork. Although included in her domestic
science curriculum, this kind of handwork evolved into what is now
industrial arts, home economics, and art education. Early progressive

thinkers in childhood education, most notably John Dewey and his student Ella Victoria Dobbs, were responsible for acknowledging the power of handwork as a method for developing human characteristics and community awareness as did sloyd, but, later, also opened possibilities for handwork as creative expression (Dobbs, 1917; 1932).

Approximately one hundred prints are kept in Emma's portfolio, most of which were published as "The Perry Pictures" in the early 1900s. Most of them are sepia toned and reflect values held of the day, mostly ennobling, moral, wholesome images. Many are of churches and other religious architecture and art. The images are reflective of pervasive values held at the time, which were influenced by John Ruskin (Efland, 1990; MacDonald, 1997). I do not know what Emma thought of these particular images or how they were introduced to her, although I do know that she liked art. She no doubt learned information about them and thought about whether or not she liked them. I suspect she liked many of them because they reflected her own spiritual beliefs. While they were not from her Perry collection, she kept two favorite reproductions in her home for as long as I can remember. One was a landscape by Corot and the other was a painting called "The Prairie is My Garden" by Harvey Dunn, a South Dakota artist. The

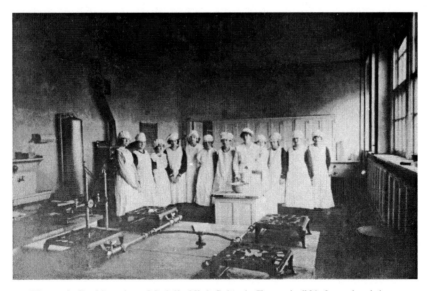

Figure 4: Cooking class, Madelia High School. Emma is fifth from the right.

latter depicts a woman dressed in simple clothing, looking out over the prairie landscape, cutting flowers with a knife. It represents both the beauty and the hardships of pioneer women.

After graduating from South Dakota State College, Emma and three friends took an excursion to Yellowstone National Park where they toured it by horse-drawn buses, the last year such transportation was used (Eyestone, 1995). After her trip, she moved to Springfield, Minnesota and taught domestic arts for two years. She later accepted a teaching position in Madelia, Minnesota where she taught high school domestic arts (see Fig. 4). There, she met a chemistry teacher, Edwin Nathaniel Johnson, a son of Swedish immigrants. They were later married on July 28, 1920 in Minneapolis. She was 30 years old. Although Emma and Edwin continued their adventures through travel for much of their married lives, Emma ended her career as a domestic science teacher and instead applied her professional knowledge to her own life as a homemaker (Eyestone, 1995). Emma and Edwin moved to Detroit Lakes, Minnesota in 1927 where they raised three children and lived for the rest of their lives. I don't know how Emma felt about having to give up her career as a teacher at this point in her life although she no doubt accepted it as simply what one did. I believe that she welcomed the opportunity to build her own family with her husband.

Although more modern conveniences were available to Emma, which she gladly used, she nevertheless maintained some of the earlier values from her childhood. She was very frugal with things of value to her, including time, money, and resources. She was a talented seamstress, making most of the coverings for her home furnishings, including the drapes and all the slipcovers. She also made her children's clothing, as well as a few things for her grandchildren. She made her grandchildren flannel nightgowns lined with parachute silk. She took great care in seeing that her children's clothes were neat, clean, and mended. She also made doll clothes for her daughter and grandchildren. My grandfather kept a large garden from which my grandmother canned most of the fruits and vegetables and put them up for the long, cold winters. I can recall going down to the basement of their house and seeing the many jars of delicious foods when I visited during the summers. I think I most appreciated the wonderful breads and cookies that Emma made and the physical and emotional warmth they provided as they baked.

Many of the values and manner of how Emma made life choices are embodied in her middle child; a daughter named Elizabeth Mae, my mother, born in 1925. Emma held high standards for herself and expected no less from her children. She was insistent that each of her three children go to college and they did. My mother attended Carleton College in Northfield, Minnesota. I visited the campus when I was deciding on where to go to college. She told me that when she was there during World War II, she was in one of the first classes where women were allowed to wear pants because it was cold and the men were at war. When she was a student there, she also took an art appreciation class. Emma gave her the set of Perry Pictures that she had used and my mother referenced them in a project of her own. Although my mother has never admitted to being a skilled artist, she taught me important things about composition and took me to art museums as a child. She also enrolled me in ballet classes when I was 5, which I continued through graduate school. I was fortunate to grow up in Washington, D.C. where there were many cultural offerings available. My mother took me to see many of them. I am certain that her appreciation and knowledge of the arts shaped my own choices in becoming an art educator.

My mother graduated from Carleton College with a Bachelor's degree in Biology in 1947. From there, she went to Washington, D. C. where she was a biologist at the National Institutes of Health (NIH). When she married my father, also a researcher at NIH, in 1952, she continued to work until she became pregnant with her first child, my brother, to whom she gave birth in 1954. At that point, she chose to end her professional career to devote her life to raising her four children.

When I chose to go to art school, my mother gave me the set of Perry Pictures. I admit that I didn't have the appreciation of their value then as I do today. I simply wanted to see if the images in the portfolio were the same as the ones I was learning about in my art history class. Some were and that was helpful. Today I use them in teaching my students about the history of art education. I lay out the pictures, carefully, and compare and contrast them with contemporary sets of images. My students do a content analysis to discover how beliefs affect our choices in what we teach. Unlike my grandmother and mother, I continue with my profession, although I married at the age of 39 and have a young child. While this life decision is different from that of my grandmother and my mother, like them, I have made my choice in relation to my family's needs and to the values and opportunities available to me in contemporary society.

When my grandmother passed away in 1995 at the age of 105, she was remembered for how much she gave to others and for her great love of children. When my daughter was born in 1996, I recall feeling sad that she would not know her great-grandmother. But I am sure now, in many respects, that she does, because of the love and care with which Emma lived by her beliefs and was able to give them to her own children and grandchildren. In giving birth to my daughter, Emma Elizabeth, I felt a strong sense of responsibility to clarify my beliefs and to live by them. My concept of time changed dramatically and I now cherish every second I have. As with the early sloyders, I hope that my daughter will understand the importance of self-reliance, caring for others, industriousness, and the importance of being able to work with one's hands. I hope that she will take pride in and understand her cultural heritage. I hope that she will be aware of and able to contribute to the community in which she lives. I hope that she will find clarity in her beliefs and will be able to live by them. And I hope that she will like art, too, and will take care of the Perry Pictures when I give them to her.

Conclusions

While my grandmother and mother were and are highly skillful in homemaking activities, including sewing, cooking, interior decorating, and budgeting, neither of them considered themselves to be artists. Although I realize that they did and do not make art in a studio, I have always been astounded that they did not think of themselves as artistic. I believe that by choosing to examine the relationships in this chapter, I have come to know why needing to resolve this discrepancy in our perceptions has been so compelling to me. I believe that what I have received in my own upbringing goes way back to the time of the early sloyders where what was most valued was the spirit of the maker more than the objects that were made.

In this chapter, I have attempted to demonstrate how the process of examining the way in which one learns, not only from more formal education, but also through family and community influences can profoundly affect our perspectives and life choices. For instance, when I was doing research on educational sloyd several years ago (Eyestone, 1989), what struck me most was how familiar much of it felt. Although I never participated in a sloyd curriculum, the values inherent in the philosophy were things that I not only understood, but also took for granted because they were a part of my upbringing. I now believe that being able to acknowledge my own cultural heritage in the process of doing historical research will bring a better understanding to the reader, and will allow me to provide more profound, unique, and creative insights in my writing. I believe that this kind of research and reflection will also manifest itself in my classroom. Taking the time to trace historical and aesthetic community influences biographically appears to me to be an important way to help students link their personal beliefs and family values to what and how they learn.

Endnote

[1] I refer to my grandmother as "Emma," her first name because the paper is written as a personal narrative. I refer to other family members by their first names for the same reason.

References

Anderson, L. (1926). *History of manual and industrial school education.* New York: D. Appleton and Company.

Dobbs, E.V. (1917). *Illustrative handwork.* New York: Macmillan.

Dobbs. E.V. (1932). *First steps in art and handwork.* New York: Macmillan Co.

Efland, A.D. (1990). *A history of art education: Intellectual and social currents in teaching the visual arts.* New York: Teachers College Press.

Eriksson, L. (1891a). The purpose of sloyd or manual training in the public school. *Sloyd or Handi-work: A Manual for the Use of Schools, 5,* 33-35. Collection the Schlesinger Library, Radcliffe College (collection number:

MC269 North Bennet Street Industrial School; box 86, folder 165).

Eyestone, E.J. (1995). Emma Slaatta Johnson. Commemorative program.

Eyestone, J.E. (1989). The influence of Swedish sloyd and its interpreters on American art education. (Doctoral dissertation, University of Missouri, 1989). *Dissertation Abstracts International, 50,* 08-A, AAD89-25281.

Eyestone, J.E. (1992). The influence of Swedish sloyd and its interpreters on American art education. *Studies in Art Education, 34*(1), 28-38.

Gaynor, E. (1987). *Scandinavia living design.* New York: Stewart, Tabori & Chang, Inc.

Hansson, K. (1966). Sloyd, prevocational, vocational, and technical education in Sweden (Doctoral dissertation, University of Missouri, 1966). *Dissertation Abstracts, 28,* 476A-477A.

Harwood, W. (1898). Sloyd: The Swedish manual-training system. *Outlook, 58,* 43-53.

Hoffman, B.B. (1892). *The sloyd system of wood working.* New York: American Book Company.

Johannesson, L. (1994). On folk art and other modernities. In E. Klein & M. Widbom (Eds.), *Swedish folk art: All tradition is change* (pp. 41-46). New York: Harry N. Abrams, Incorporated.

Klein, B. & Widbom, M. (Eds.) (1994). *Swedish folk art: All tradition is change.* New York: Harry N. Abrams, Incorporated.

Larsson, G. (1893). Sloyd for elementary schools contrasted with the Russian system of manual training. *National Education Association addresses and proceedings, 31,* 155-161.

MacDonald, B.L. (1997). The Perry Magazine for School and Home (1898-1906): An analysis of its historical location within the schoolroom decoration and picture study movements. In P. Bolin & A. Anderson (Eds.), *History of art education: Proceedings of the Third Penn State International Symposium* (pp. 404-420). University Park, PA: The Pennsylvania State University.

Salomon, O. (1911). *The theory of educational sloyd (4th ed.).* Boston: Silver, Burdett & Co.

Sterner, M. (1939). *Homecrafts in Sweden.* The Tithe House Leigh-on-Sea: F. Lewis Publishers.

Thompson, M. (1983). *Superbly Swedish: Recipes and traditions.* Iowa City, IA: Penfield Press.

chapter

15

Remote Control: Performing Memory and Cultural History

Charles R. Garoian

...the speech act is at the same time a use *of* language and an operation performed *on* it.
Michel de Certeau, *The Practice of Everyday Life*

In making invisible histories visible, art students can use performance art as a live memory and cultural history collage. The conjunctions of disparate images, ideas, and actions in performance artworks function as a form of research and critique of socially and historically determined representations; one that provides possibilities for multicultural and cross-disciplinary curriculum and instruction in art education. The process of providing testimony of one's cultural past, and witnessing those of others, represents interpersonal and intercultural research that exposes knowledge that would otherwise remain unknown, untold, and unmarked by the dominant culture (Felman 1987, 1992). Such content enables political agency, critical citizenship, and a sense of community among art students who learn to validate knowledge from their families, neighborhoods, and communities.

My own development as an artist and teacher, for example, was greatly influenced by the stories my parents told. The way in which they worked and played with images and ideas were liberating in the context of our daily struggles. The strategies which they used to define their lives inspired what I *say* and *do* in my art and in my teaching. My cultural work as an artist and educator is built on the aesthetic substance of my parents' ideas and actions; on their ways of saying and doing things on our farm and in our home; on their stories about the "Old Country" and the horrors of genocide which they experienced as children; on how they constructed their lives and identities as Armenian emigrants in America. In addition to life with my parents, I have been influenced by my siblings, the neighborhood and community in which I grew up, and the schools I attended. Local, national and worldwide events reported through the mass media, and the experiences of popular culture, have also affected who I am and where I come from.

Remembering, reclaiming, representing the past is a form of critical inquiry and performance; a speech act that enables the play and disruption of established cultural forces and representations, according to cultural historian Michel de Certeau (1984, pp. 18, 33). Such a process can yield significant content for art education: images, ideas, and actions that students can use to acknowledge the significance of their cultural backgrounds; to critique the dominant codes of schooling; to construct their own identities; and, to create new cultural metaphors that are relevant to their lives in the contemporary world.

In what follows, I describe the performance of memory and cultural history in *Remote Control*, a work that I performed in 1998 at the Cleveland Performance Art Festival, and the HERE space and Ohio Theater in New York City. While doing so, I deconstruct the various components of the performance to illustrate how it functions as a live memory and cultural history collage. Its disjunctive construction relates to the ways in which my parents constructed meaning through work and play in their everyday lives. Their stories and playful activities served as "tactics" to subvert and transform the oppressive conditions of emigrant life and the subsistent living on our small raisin vineyard in Fresno, California. According to de Certeau (1984), "a *tactic* is an art of the weak" (p. 37). It functions as a way of operating in everyday life that transforms cultural oppression. My parents tactics "insinuate[d] into the [American] system...ways of 'dwelling'" in its place or language (p. 30). In doing so, they found "ways of using the constraining order of the place or of the language [to establish] within it a degree of plurality and creativity" (p. 30).

De Certeau's notion of insinuation relates to scientist philosopher Robert Crease's use of "argumentative analogies" as "tool[s] whereby a structured set of relations present in one area [are] introduced into another" (p. 76). Crease claims the purpose for such conjunctions in scientific experiments is to evoke the "play of nature" whereby each set of relations begs the question of the other. He argues the necessity for such interventions in the creation of new artistic and scientific concepts similar to de Certeau's "degree[s] of plurality and creativity." Furthermore, de Certeau's tactics and Crease's argumentative analogies correspond with cultural historian Johan Huizinga's (1950) two main liberating characteristics of play. First, "that it [play] is free, is in fact freedom"; and second, that play enables "stepping out of 'real' life into a temporary sphere of activity with a disposition all of its own" (p. 8).

Disrupting the space of dominant culture by introducing argumentative analogies to make it function in another register is similar to the "rupturing" and "contentious" theories of educational critics Paulo Friere (1993), Henry Giroux (1993), Maxine Greene (1988), and Carol Becker (1996) whose critical pedagogies resist cultural domination through radical democratic practices in education. Correspondingly, personal memory and cultural history are used by performance artists like Tim Miller (*Fruit Cocktail*) to challenge homophobia; the Guerrilla Girls in their urban interventions to critique the politics of gender; and Guillermo Gómez-Peña whose intercultural discourse in works like *Border Brujo* provide a politics of resistance through performance art.

Similar to the practices of these artists and theorists, the tactics that my parents performed in everyday life enabled them to attain political agency in American culture. The lessons of their struggle continue to serve as the pedagogical background for my cultural work as an art educator and performance artist. Similar to their "ways of operating," I use a collage of tactics in *Remote Control* (Figure 1) as a pedagogical "strategy" to critique Guy Debord's (1995) spectacle of mass media culture and Jean Baudrillard's (1984) simulacra. Unlike the lack of position against which the oppressed deploy tactics to overturn, a strategy is a "rationalization [that] seeks first of all to distinguish its 'own' place, that is, the place of its own power and will" (de Certeau,

p. 36). My performance of cultural ideas, images, actions, and myths in *Remote Control* represents a strategy for empowerment; the practice of critical citizenship that will enable my political agency within contemporary culture.

Remote Control (1998): Concept, Inquiry, Cultural Commentary

Figure 1: *Remote Control* detail

Remote Control critiques the inscription of my body by television culture. A TV is strapped to my back mounted on a specially designed and modified backpack. My words, sounds, and gestures are governed by televised images and their messages. What is being remotely controlled in the performance is not the television, but my body. In a monologue I talk about seeing TV for the first time; how it replaced family activities and religious rituals; how it disrupted both work and play while growing up; and, how it *taught* me to look, behave, walk, and to speak. In my performance, I carry the burden of that experience on my back. I re-member, re-consider, re-present my television memories from the perspective of my body. To resist domination by the mass media, I move, speak, gesture, and make sounds. I physically exhaust my body to make it explicit; to expose its absent, hidden character. My purpose is to question the *remote control of my body* by the spectacle of television culture. In what follows, I provide excerpts of *Remote Control* to illustrate how it functions as a memory and cultural history performance.

Description of Performance: Actions, Visuals, Text, Sound, and Time

00:00 Part I: Charles walks out into a dark performance space sans shirt, reaches for a trouble light and switches it on to reveal it hanging over the torch of the Statue of Liberty. He turns around, walks down stage towards the audience and delivers the first monologue while pacing from stage left, to center, to right, and back again.

> *I was eight years old. It was pitch black outside. My father and I were barbecuing out in the yard, on our farm, next to the vineyard. The sweet aroma of lamb permeated the night air; throughout the entire neighborhood.*

As he begins to deliver his next line, Charles turns and walks up stage where he grabs the trouble light from its hook over the window shade and returns with it down stage holding the light with his right hand over his head to illuminate the stage, a posture that mimics the Statue of Liberty.

> *Father walked over to the shed and pulled out the trouble light, the one he would often use to repair the tractor whenever it broke down in the middle of the night. He brought it over to the barbecue pit to see if the meat was done, to see if it was ready to eat. When he switched on the light, I caught a glimpse of the large star tattooed on his right upper arm.*

01:03 Charles reaches over and touches his right upper arm as if the memory of his father's tattoo was inscribed on his own body.

> *He caught me looking at it, he caught me staring. He admonished me never to mark my body the way he had done. Out of embarrassment, I looked away into the dark trying to figure out what I'd said to offend him, to make him react the way that he did.*

Charles pauses, then continues.

> *Just then Mother called me into the house to bathe before dinner. I*

*ran in immediately to get away from the situation with my father. I
jumped into the tub where she bathed me. Then she had me stand on
the toilet seat where she toweled me off. As she was drying my legs,
she pointed to the two large birth marks directly across from each
other on the front of my thighs.*

Charles reaches down and points to the center of each thigh.
   *"Distinguishing marks," she said. God given distinguishing marks
that she would use to find me should I ever get lost or kidnapped.*

02:05 Charles pauses again, pulls on the cord of the trouble light to
reel it in, and adjusts its length so that it hangs six inches above the
floor. As the light castes a large shadow of his body onto the back wall,
he continues his monologue.
   *My mother was kidnapped as a child. She was taken from my
grandmother's arms while the two of them were in exodus during the
1915 Armenian Genocide. They were walking along a path when a
Turkish soldier rode up on horseback, grabbed my mother from my
grandmother's arms, and rode off into the distance. Horrified over
the ordeal, my grandmother fell to her knees and began to slap her
thighs lamenting, crying out, begging for God's mercy. All the while,
she kept her eyes fixed on the diminishing image of the soldier
carrying my mother away; as they got smaller, and smaller, and
smaller, and smaller until they were a dot on the horizon. She fixed
her gaze on that dot until...it disappeared. She still didn't give up
hope. She scanned the horizon line back and forth, back and forth,
back and forth, hoping, praying until finally the dot reappeared and
got larger, and larger, and larger, and larger. The soldier returned
and placed my mother back in my grandmother's arms and told her:
"I couldn't bear to take a crying child from its mother.*

04:05 Part II: Charles straps the TV to his back and plugs its cord into
the receptacle of the trouble light which is suspended from the ceiling.
As the brightly lit blank screen of the TV begins to beam out at the
audience, Charles takes the trouble light in hand and stands looking in
the opposite direction towards a large eye chart projected on the back
wall of the performance space. The letters on the chart repeatedly spell
"H-E-G-E-M-O-N-Y-O-F-T-H-E-E-Y-E" to parody the privileging and
domination of the eye by the spectacle of the mass media. For each

segment of the eye test, and while mimicking Liberty's torch hold with the trouble light in one hand and covering his eye with the other, Charles pivots his body so that the TV is aimed left, center, right stage, then back again. In doing so, he subverts the viewers' expectations of a fixed frame of reference; he yields, then denies the viewers gaze and fixation on the screen; and, his eccentric actions reveal his body's inscription by the schizophrenia of TV's mass mediated images.

04:28 An audiotape of Charles's voice, amplified in the performance space, proctors the eye examination while a sound track of electronic music plays in the background.

06:10 Charles segues into Part III of the performance by recapitulating his movements and mimicking "O-F-T-H-E-E-Y-E" aloud to create an historical structure among the disparate elements of the performance. He continues to repeat his actions and soliloquy throughout the second monologue which is broadcast in the performance space by an audio system while the blank screen of the TV on his back begins a flickering flurry of channel surfing images. The broadcast monologue tells of the eerie circumstances surrounding the first time Charles witnessed television at 12 years of age.

11:15 Charles continues the soliloquy "O-F-T-H-E-E-Y-E" as he gradually halts his movements. He carefully releases a trouble light to hang down from the ceiling just above the floor. As he gradually resumes his movements, the light fixture, which also serves as a receptacle for the TV cord, begins to sway casting large shadows of his TV mounted body onto the back wall. A flickering flurry of channel surfing images from Part III shift to a large image of Charles's lips filling the TV screen. When the lips bellow *Hey you!,* the refrain of the third monologue, Charles begins forcibly twisting, jerking his torso back and forth, looking out into the audience. From one side of his body to the other, he attempts to locate the source of the voice. Is the voice calling out to Charles? Is Charles looking for the person who is being admonished by the TV lips? Is Charles looking for himself as the perpetrator?

Figure 2: *Remote Control* detail

The pronoun "you" references himself and each member of the audience simultaneously thus chastising all for their acquiescence to TV culture. Meanwhile, the trouble light jerks and sways according to Charles's movements and continues to cast large shadows of his moving body against the back wall. When the refrain ends and the monologue begins, he spins around and runs back and forth between stage right and left swinging the trouble light behind him as he goes (Figure 2).

11:45 Part IV: The admonishing lips gesticulate as they enunciate every word of the third monologue.
HEY! HEY YOU! HEY THERE! HEY!
YAH, YOU! I'M TALKING TO YOU!

In the kitchen, in the living room, you watch it, it watches you. In the bedrooms and bathrooms, you control it, it controls you. You're surrounded, it's ubiquitous, it's everywhere. Colliding pictures and sound bites terrorize your thoughts. Contiguous images construct your identity. Four, six, eight, ten, twelve hours a day. You're anesthetized, numb, indifferent. You once learned by scanning,

physically turning your head. Maneuvering, you continually reposi-
tioned yourself. You wanted to see what you were looking at, you
said. Your gaze is now fixed, you no longer have to move. Without
effort, you look, but are blind to the world.

Charles repeats his running, bends over, puts his hands on his thighs,
and catches his breath with loud sighs. The TV on his back moves to
the rhythm of his breathing.
HEY! HEY YOU! HEY THERE! HEY!
YAH, YOU! I'M TALKING TO YOU!

Charles begins forcibly twisting, jerking his torso back and forth,
looking out into the audience. From one side of his body to the other,
he attempts to locate the source of the voice until the refrain ends.
Then he spins around and runs back and forth between stage right and
left swinging the trouble light behind him as he goes.
Packard Bell, Motorola, RCA, Zenith commercials whetted your
appetite. You wanted a console model, not a portable, and finally
got one in your house. It replaced family activities, religious rituals,
time with your friends. Work, play, and pray were disrupted as you
sat and gazed at the box. You learned to look, behave, walk, and
speak like...like...like...like...like. You saw it for the first time just
after Elvis made his debut on Ed Sullivan. The reasons for his pelvic
gyrations now seem rather obvious. Necessary movement to com-
pensate for disembodied experience. You laid on the sofa while
watching him perform Jailhouse Rock. When you got older, you
danced your ass off at Big Bob's Rock n' Roll. You wanted to experi-
ence your body, you forgot you had one, you said.

13:19 Charles stops his running, bends over, puts his hands on his
thighs, and catches his breath with loud sighs. The TV on his back
moves to the rhythm of his breathing.
HEY! HEY YOU! HEY THERE! HEY!
YAH, YOU! I'M TALKING TO YOU!

Charles repeats forcibly twisting, jerking his torso back and forth,
looking out into the audience. From one side of his body to the other,
he attempts to locate the source of the voice until the refrain ends.
Then he spins around and runs back and forth between stage right and

left swinging the trouble light behind him as he goes.

Outside intervention going on in your own house. Held hostage, you sit in the dark and attend to schizophrenic images. You've become accustomed to experiencing reality vicariously. Yours is an immaculate perception, a sanitary life. You travel the far reaches of the world, visit other cultures, past, present, future. You are there, but not there. You see dirt, but don't get dirty. You see sweat, but sit in your air conditioned environment. You see hunger, but walk to the refrigerator for a snack. You see pestilence, but have a team of doctors and pharmacy at hand. No more anger, fear, anxiety, worry, happiness, peace, or joy. No more to think about and nothing to feel. The spectacle is your life's blood.

Charles stops his running, bends over, puts his hands on his thighs, and catches his breath with loud sighs. The TV on his back moves to the rhythm of his breathing.

HEY! HEY YOU! HEY THERE! HEY!
YAH, YOU! I'M TALKING TO YOU!

Charles repeats forcibly twisting, jerking his torso back and forth, looking out into the audience. From one side of his body to the other, he attempts to locate the source of the voice until the refrain ends. Then he spins around and runs back and forth between stage right and left swinging the trouble light behind him as he goes.

As its light directs your eyes, you enjoy being interrogated. As gaze returns gaze, you're seduced by its arrogance. You sit passively, watching, listening, acquiescing to its demands. As it placates, you no longer confront your problems or work them out. You're part of a family, but everyone seems a stranger. You merely inhabit the same time and space. You are present, yet absent. You join in, but feel alone. You're spoken to, but rarely speak. When you do, you never make eye contact. Your eyes are glazed over. Your eyelids are dried in their sockets. You look, but see nothing.

Charles stops his running, bends over, puts his hands on his thighs, and catches his breath with loud sighs. The TV on his back moves to the rhythm of his breathing.

HEY! HEY YOU! HEY THERE! HEY!
YAH, YOU! I'M TALKING TO YOU!

Charles repeats forcibly twisting, jerking his torso back and forth, looking out into the audience. From one side of his body to the other, he attempts to locate the source of the voice until the refrain ends. Then he spins around and runs back and forth between stage right and left swinging the trouble light behind him as he goes (Figure 3).

MTV, Court TV, Church TV, The Late Night Show. Days of Our Lives, As the World Turns, Wheel of Fortune, Jeopardy, Football, Baseball, Basketball, Hockey, Wrestling. Chicago Hope, ER, NYPD Blue, Law & Order, Seinfeld, Ellen, Frasier. Oprah, Sally Jesse Raphael, Jerry Springer. The six o'clock news, CNN, The Food Channel, the Weather Channel. Nike, Coke, Pepsi, Nissan, Toyota, AT&T, RotoRooter. More than you need to sustain yourself, everything to indulge your desires. You consume heaps of culture, but your production is immobilized. You witness, but give no testimony. You see it all, but say nothing. You read, but can't grasp anything.

16:26 Charles stops his running, bends over, puts his hands on his thighs, and catches his breath with loud sighs. The TV on his back moves to the rhythm of his breathing.

HEY! HEY YOU! HEY THERE! HEY!
YAH, YOU! I'M TALKING TO YOU!

Figure 3: *Remote Control* detail

Charles repeats forcibly twisting, jerking his torso back and forth, looking out into the audience. From one side of his body to the other, he attempts to locate the source of the voice until the refrain ends. Then he spins around and runs back and forth between stage right and left swinging the trouble light behind him as he goes.

Are you object or are you subject; are you spectacle or spectator? Is what you're looking at, what you see? You are marked, yet you're uncertain of your identity. The weight bears down on your back, yet you feel no burden. You are not a specimen, you are not a corpse. Hey! Your body's here, you can speak. Hey you! Your body's here, you can gesture. Hey there! Your body's here, you can make sounds. Hey! Your body's here, you can see. Yah, you! Your body's here. I'm talking to you! Your body's here. Hey! Your body's here; yah, your body's here. Your body's here, your body's here, your body's here. You body seer, you body seer, you body seer, you brought us here, you brought us here, you brought us here, you bought us here, you bought us here, you bought us here.

17:25 Part V: Charles stops his running, bends over, puts his hands on his thighs, and catches his breath with loud sighs. The TV on his back moves to the rhythm of his breathing. He turns around to face the audience. Illuminated by the hanging trouble light and breathless, he bends over and begins making loud sounds by repeatedly slapping his thighs with his hands as he repeats the following phrase three times.

...he pulled the trouble light from the shed to see if the meat was done.

He unbuckles his belt and lowers his pants to expose two large bandages located on both thighs while repeating the following.

...he pulled the trouble light from the shed to see if the meat was done.

He reaches for the trouble light and illuminates the bandages. He turns from side to side, peeling back each of the bandages to expose the birthmarks. As they are nonexistent, he massages the area as if to soothe a memory.

...he pulled the trouble light from the shed to see if the meat was done.

He turns off the trouble light, pivots his body around to expose the snow, white noise of the video monitor to the audience. In the dark of the performance space, the flickering image appears to float in mid air as he gently sways his body back and forth.

19:45 Charles unplugs the video monitor from the trouble light receptacle and drops the chord onto the floor with a thud to end the performance.

Construction of Signifiers

In Part I, the outlined image of the Statue of Liberty on the window shade suggests at least four possible readings: first, as a pedagogical chart to interject the question of civil liberties when challenging the body's cultural inscription; second, to problematize the concepts of freedom and enlightenment signified by her torch with the "trouble light"; third, to provide a backdrop for the window portion of the second monologue that tells of seeing TV for the first time; and fourth, to signify the ocular occlusion manifested by the gaze of TV culture.

In the first monologue, the paradox of my father's tattoo admonition, and my mother's attention to my birthmarks, suggests what de Certeau (1984) refers to as a "memory tattooed by oppression, a past inscribed on the body" (p. 32). This memory metaphorically links my mother's "kidnapping" with that of my own body by TV culture. Signifying the ideological authority of linear perspective, the "enemy" snatches the child from its mother and vanishes into the line of the horizon. The transformative power my grandmother's vision, manifested through her hope and perseverance, suggests the re-claiming of the abducted body from the body politic.

In Part II, I proctor to myself an eye examination to check my fluency, to re-member and re-claim the power of my grandmother's vision as my inheritance. Ironically, as I test its facility, my gaze is fixed on the text of eye chart. Assuming that I am not oblivious to its message, the chart contains a dual reading: on the one hand, *H-E-G-E-M-O-N-Y-O-F-T-H-E-E-Y-E* can be interpreted literally as the privileging and dominance of ocular culture; and, on the other hand, it can be interpreted as a warning to resist the eye's hegemony, the culturally constructed methods by which it frames and represents reality.

In Part III, my repeated reading of the exam text with a TV strapped to my back echoed by my mechanical movements suggests my body's inscription and behavioral conditioning by TV culture; the transformation of my cyborg identity. Conversely, I "mimic" the stereotyping of my body by TV culture to expose, examine, and critique its dominant pedagogy. My memory and history with TV (the second monologue), the mysterious shadows flickering from the light of TV inside the neighbor's house (a reference to Plato's Allegory of the Cave that will be discussed later), the way in which it disrupted family life are performed to counter, resist the power of its spectacle.

In Part IV, the *Hey You!* monologue exhorts, provokes, stirs, and agitates the anesthetized eye, mind, and body of the subject; implicating me and the audience, as uncritical consumers of TV culture. Frenzied, I run back and forth with the TV on my back to exhaust myself; to shift the concept of "consumption" to my body by "spending" its energy; by making a spectacle of myself to resist the foregrounding of my body, its absence by the spectacle of TV. Paradoxically, as I run back and forth to find my body, my self, and my identity, I chase the moving shadows of my body cast by the trouble light as if seeking truth in an illusory image. A modern version of Plato's "Allegory of the Cave," I twist back and forth at each exhortation of *Hey You!* hoping to find in my delusional state of mind whoever is calling me out. I run back and forth chasing the shadows of my body as if to capture the reality of my identity (Plato, 1960, pp. 227-231).

In Part V, recapitulations are performed as a strategy to construct a "history" of the performance from within itself; to give it a compositional structure. For example, the soliloquy, *...he pulled the trouble light from the shed to see if the meat was done,* links the end of the performance with the beginning and transfers the lamb barbecue metaphor to the inspection of my birthmarks, and the "marking" of my body by TV culture. When I expose my thighs to reveal large bandages, I do so to confirm the existence of those markings. As I peel back the bandages, they are not evident. Were they merely a figment of my imagination? Am I to assume that my body's inscription by TV culture was imagined or is its presence an insidious, stealth phenomenon, hidden and repressed in my consciousness? In the end, the floating eye, picture of the TV in the dark represents a ruse, a tactic that I use to subvert the absolute conditions of TV; its stationary position as a cultural artifact in our homes, and the resoluteness of its message.

Implications Of Memory And Cultural History For Art Education Practice

Students' memory and cultural history performances introduce hitherto hidden and unknown content in the classroom that can problematize and critique academic culture. Using de Certeau's tactics and Crease's argumentative analogies, students can learn to insinuate or introduce the content of their cultural backgrounds in three contexts. First, in the art curriculum the introduction of memory and cultural history enables them to expose, examine, and critique cultural inscription in order to re-claim their bodies and to construct their identities through art.

The exposure and introduction of such content enables students to examine and critique the character of their lives and to apply the knowledge and insights gained from such self-reflexive endeavors toward the creation of ideas, images, and myths that are significant to their construction of identity. In an academic and mass-mediated world where they are treated as objects, they learn to use their memories, cultural histories, and bodies to construct and perform their subjectives as strategies to resistance cultural objectification and assimilation.

Second, by crossing disciplinary boundaries, students learn to insinuate and interconnect the contents of their lives, with their artworks, and with the disparate disciplines of academic culture. In doing so, art, mathematics, science, literature, foreign languages, and other classes across the curriculum, take on a personal significance when experienced through the lenses of students' cultural perspectives.

Third, the performance of memory and cultural history enables students to experience the cultural perspectives of their peers and to gain a respect for their cultural differences. This intercultural dimension of their performance work is essential in their learning to build cooperative and collaborative links between themselves, their families, neighborhoods, and the communities in which they live. As students challenge socially and historically constructed assumptions through memory and cultural performances in the art classroom, they learn the art of critical citizenship, a lesson that is necessary for their attainment of political agency within contemporary culture.

References

Baudrillard, J. (1984). The precession of simulacra. In B. Wallis (Ed.), *Art after modernism: Rethinking representation* (pp. 253-281). New York: The New Museum of Contemporary Art.

Becker, C. (1996). *Zones of contention: Essays on art, institutions, gender, and anxiety.* Albany: The State University of New York.

Debord, G. (1995). *The society of the spectacle.* New York: Zone.

de Certeau, M. (1984). *The practice of everyday life* (S. Rendall, Trans.). Berkeley: The University of California.

Felman, S. (1987). *Jacques Lacan and the adventure of insight: Psychoanalysis in contemporary culture.* Cambridge: Harvard University.

Felman, S. (1992). Education and crisis, or the vicissitudes of teaching. In S. Felman & D. Laub (Eds.), Testimony: *Crises of witnessing in literature, psychoanalysis, and history* (pp. 1-56). New York: Routledge.

Freire, P. (1993). *Pedagogy of the oppressed.* New York: Continuum.

Giroux, H.A. (1993). *Border crossings: Cultural workers and the politics of education.* New York: Routledge.

Greene, M. (1988). *The dialectic of freedom.* New York: Teachers College, Columbia University.

Huizinga, J. (1950). *Homo ludens: A study of the play-element in culture.* Boston: The Beacon Press.

Plato. (1960). *The republic of Plato* (F.M. Cornford, Trans.). London: Oxford University.

chapter

16

Guerrero Family Art Traditions

Mary Stokrocki

Look in any *Arizona Republic* newspaper around the end of October
and you will find photos of magnificent puppets for the annual *Dia de
los Muertos* (Day of the Dead) celebration that takes place on the first
and second of November.[1] I first saw the puppets at the Heard Museum
several years ago. These 10 feet tall smiling skeletons, operated by a
person hidden underneath the cloth body, strolled around the crowd
and greeted visitors. One giant skeleton puppet (Don Gueso—Grandfather Death) put its arm around my husband. I'll never forget how his
face flushed with embarrassment. Most Euro-Americans would be
uncomfortable with such an embrace. For Mexican-Americans, who
now refer to themselves as Chicanos or Chicanas for ethnic pride, this
friendly caress is a traditional reminder of that ultimate kinship system
that we all will eventually join—death. These fascinating puppets and
masks were designed by one of Arizona's favorite artists, Zarco
Guerrero. Dina Lopez, Executive Director of *Xicanindio Artes*,
Arizona's oldest ethnic arts organization, praises his multiple talents.
She exclaims, "Zarco is the state's premier artist. His work is great"
(Amparano, 1997, p. A6). Zarco creates art with his entire family and
extends it into the community.

The Euro-American modern nuclear family with its element of privacy
tends to make people isolated and lonely. Slater (1976) feels that more

interaction among people and especially family members is necessary for both mental health and stronger communities. Many families now consist of extended members, often the results of remarriage. Some families even include pets as part of their household. Family art as a way to unite people becomes more important since it can extend into social, religious, and educational aspects of a community. Folklorists and some art therapists write on family art traditions, mostly from a Euro-American point of view. More descriptions about how people from other cultures celebrate their family artmaking traditions are needed. In the chapter, I seek to explain the concept of family art and describe through oral history methods[2] how one Chicano family makes and performs art in the community, thereby extending its traditions.

What is Family Art?

According to Cutting-Baker (1976), family art is a verbal, written, ritual, or visual representation of a family culture. Family art can be a form of entertainment or a craft; it can become fine art. We also associate family art with household spaces (Bachelard, 1969). These spaces may be intimate and/or grand. Family art is more than an artifact in a room or a house. It often helps form an environment. Family art also recalls the past and projects itself into a future (Jones,

1959). Some families have homes that resemble living museums that are filled with pictures and collectibles. These material things convey a family's unique personality and cultural identity (Mathiesen, 1982). Other families present their homes as fashion statements from magazines with little family uniqueness. Still other family homes are filled with family treasures: mementos and reliquaries of friends and careers that exhibit family character. Visual family traditions include such artworks as family portraits, photographic albums, and children's drawings.

Several scholars have documented the childhood effects of family art rituals. Nesbit (1913) re-creates miniature cities from childhood memories made from household items. Lindgren (1963) relates fond memories of decorating a family room for her birthday. Ritenoir (1983) studies how families and personal relationships affect some artists. Some artifacts associated with family art have to do with mourning or loss. Examples are quilts, cards, or altars in memory of loved ones. Even garden structures and dollhouses can be enlivened with family art. D'Amico (1954) describes the teaching and benefits of families making art together in his program at The Metropolitan Museum of Art. This program, in which parents and children make art together, continues today (Silberstein-Storfer, 1982). Family art celebrates domestic values while it functions to enhance hospitality and community. In doing so, it fuses private and public domains (Becker, 1982). The community, often seen as a large family, encourages more interactions between local families. According to Hyde (1983), the purposes of family art are to exchange ideas, enhance our world, and expand on our common traditions. For Pacey (1989), family art can nurture its members as creative people, enhance their choices, and encourage new artistic syntheses. In the following section, I explore the changing art traditions of one Chicano family, while emphasizing the functions of family art.

An Oral History of the Guerrero Family Art-Making Traditions

The Guerrero family, who settled in Mesa, Arizona before the Mormons, always made some kind of traditional art. For example, Zarco Guerrero's great-great-grandfather was a Tepehuano Indian who worked with leather and his grandfather was a sign artist. Zarco, born in 1952, was the only boy and youngest of four children. Eventually he assumed the nickname "Zarco," meaning "clear-eyed one." (His eyes are more of a gray-green than brown.) Zarco's early childhood influences can be traced back to his mother and father. His mother was a seamstress, who made clothes for his flamenco-dancing sisters. Zarco admitted that he is keenly aware of fabric and costumes because of her influence. His dad was a commercial artist and formally-trained portrait painter. Zarco intently watched him draw and followed his dad to painting classes. Zarco's first painted his classmates' portraits. He remembers, "I found that capturing the likeness of an individual is very difficult." Elementary school formally offered few art experiences, except making school posters. In high school, he took the regular art courses, but was more interested in wrestling at that time. However, he soon became the class artist. People always told him that "he would become an artist, like his dad." These constant reminders reinforced his interests in art.

After high school graduation in 1970, Zarco went to New York to find an art school. Here he visited galleries and museums instead. Later, he traveled to Europe to observe the art scene. In Mexico City he found his trade. He visited Mexico's famous sculptor Francisco Zuniga who felt that too many people imitated his style. Consequently, he sent Zarco to work in the De Aguila bronze foundry from age 20-25. Zarco worked here alongside other artists and learned how to make molds and casts. This was one of his best learning experiences. In 1975, he had his first one person show, which featured bronzes of suffering people. However, he found that carving masks was more profitable than bronze casting. Despite little formal art training, he considered himself a sculptor.

In 1975-76, his reputation as a mask carver heightened when he won a prestigious Japanese Fellowship from the National Endowment for the Arts. With NEA's support, he studied master mask makers in Kyoto for a year. To learn more about mask making traditions, he traveled to Indonesia and China. He displayed masks from Japan, Mexico, and Alaska, as well as those he made, throughout his house. His living room features several of Zarco's incredible pieces (see Figure 2). The mask continues to dominate Zarco's work. He explains, "There's a mysticism and spirituality about masks. Their power and attraction comes from the linkage with the ancient past and the animal kingdom." He usually creates human figural masks, but he constructed a jaguar mask for his younger son to

perform in at school (see Figure 3). The jaguar is an Aztec symbol of strength and power.[3] Zarco explains, "My initial inspiration was my cultural heritage. Now I interpret the world. I thank my teachers in Mexico, Japan, and Alaska for their advice and I give back to children what I have learned."

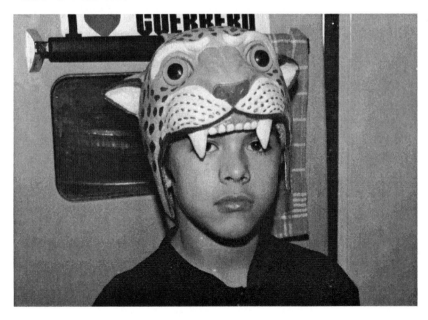

Zarco first carves giant puppet heads and masks out of foam, then casts them in fiberglass, and finally paints them with acrylics. He operates the puppets with lightweight PVC pipes and levers inside the form and adds assorted fabrics for costumes. He explains, "I make them during the winter in my backyard studio."

The family traveled to Alaska four times to see the wonderful tribal carvings of the Northwest Coast Native Americans. Zarco wanted to study Alaskan Native American carving techniques. He also noticed that his youngest son, Tizoc, was impressed with the stories of the raven, wolf, and the eagle and wanted to make masks himself. Zarco believes that families should travel together to experience these great traditional art forms and gain new insights into different cultures.

Zarco's Brazilian wife, Carmen, is the family musician. She sings and plays the piano. In fact, she can play almost any instrument. She runs the popular family band, "Zum, Zum, Zum." They perform at the Day of the Dead events with another Chicano family of dancers. This family, The Vanek's, performs as *calacas encantrada,* which are enchanting skeletons that represent rejuvenation. Carmen also conducts residencies where she teaches music and how to make instruments out of pop cans. Rain sticks are also made for praying. She

reads Brazilian stories, and demonstrates how to make animal masks, calculate inches of rain, and participate in Brazilian chants. Carmen creates her own beaded jewelry as well. She displays the colorful collection in her bedroom (see Figure 4). She confesses, "I dream about the designs and use bead work as a healing art from stress. It is my private art."[4] The Guerrero family, not only adheres to traditions, they break from them, inventing new ways of exploring their cultural beliefs. For example, Zarco's oldest son, Quetzel, a high school student at the New School for the Arts, plays guitar and directs his own band. Contemporary popular culture fuses with tradition. Quetzel designs logos for his band, *Gato Loco* (Crazy Cat), and his break dancing group. One logo reads, "Hey B-Boy! Why don't you bust?" (Figure 5). Quetzel believes that schools should hold communal events. He stated, "Break dancing is the ultimate art form in getting kids involved! Kids don't realize how much they have in common." Quetzel, describes his father as "flexible and curious about every challenge." He adds, "Dad taught me not to limit myself and to experiment." Quetzel is changing the family art traditions.

Although Zarco is not crazy about break dancing, he understands that his son needs it as a form of socialization, physical release, ritual sport, and a means of expression. Zarco explains, "The kids battle through dance and movement for several hours a week. They literally challenge themselves and others and stay in excellent shape." Zarco explains that some of Quetzel's best friends are other Native American children, such as those who belong to the Salt River Pima tribe and do ceremonial running. Zarco confides, "My children are absorbing my skills through osmosis but I also want them to be trained by other mentors to make them more rounded."

The younger Guerrero children just made their musical debut at school. Tizoc, who is eight-years-old, told me that he was the dragon-head in the Chinese New Year, Dragon Dance Performance at their school. His 6-year-old sister, Zarina, dressed in her favorite princess costume and played the violin for me. Zarco reflects, "Kids pick up your habits. They will speak the same artistic language that you speak." He wants to give them a sense of hard work, self-determination, and accomplishment.

Other children benefit from Zarco's fatherly advice. Zarco runs plaster mask making workshops for the Phoenix Boys and Girls Club of Metropolitan Phoenix after school in predominately Chicano areas. The children love to work in teams, cast their faces to make masks, and paint them. The primary objective of the workshop is for youth to acquire knowledge about Meso-American myths, rituals, and symbols and their significance in contemporary Chicano culture. Judy Butzine, Coordinator of the Art Web component of the Boys and Girls Club, contracts Zarco to conduct mask making workshops and praises his efforts:

> Not only does Zarco teach the meaning and art of mask making, he encourages these same youths to design and make mask pole *ofrendas* that they later carry in procession during the *Dia de los Muertos* festivities. Children inscribe prayers in both Spanish and English on satin ribbons that hang from the mask poles. These ribbons blow in the wind sending those messages up to the heavens. (J. Butzine, personal communication, January 30, 1998)

These kids, many who are at-risk, need to learn how to develop a sense of worth, an easygoing temperament, and a positive relationship with at least one adult (Huang, 1998).

The Guerrero house is always full of artistic friends who seem to have had a lasting impact on his children and his Chicano community. Musicians, actors, and visual artists flock to the house with much inspiration and gaiety. Zarco admits, "I love collaborating with other people! We need to express who we really are" (Amparano, 1997, p. A1). For example, to preserve their mask making family heritage, Zarco, his dad, and friends transformed a modest townhouse into a museum in Alamos, Sonora, Mexico. In Phoenix, Zarco works to preserve his Chicano heritage through one-act or community performances. He also cast a bronze memorial to Cesar Chavez, the famous farm leader and liberator. This 8-foot sculpture, commissioned by the Phoenix government, is the first city monument in Chicano history. Chicano community artist and graduate student, Lisza Jaurigue, discusses Zarco's influence on the community, "Zarco rallies the Chicano community to participate in Chicano cultural events (see Figure 6). He provides a mission for our disenfranchised family, whose problems are not alleviated. He reaffirms traditional values that are lacking in society" (L. Jaurigue, personal communication, January 27, 1998). Zarco summarizes, "I want to make art that affects people's lives, which is a reward in itself. It's a tool for social change and sharing cultural experiences."

Conclusion

This portrait of a Chicano family captures some of its changing spaces, traditions, and commitment to the greater community. Family art, for the Guerreros, becomes an unselfish gift. This gift is a memorial to his Mexican heritage as well as other cultural traditions the family admires. Family members offer their art to others, both inside and outside the family, to celebrate life and friendship. The Guerrero family masks, puppets, and performances lift and expand our spirits. Their art unifies their ancestors, immediate family, and extends into the communal family. In this case, family art has successfully fused the private and public domains and it has adapted new ideas while rooting itself in ancestral artistic practices.

Endnotes

[1]This annual rite traditionally features life that embraces death. The most important part is the celebration of families bonding in honor of their ancestors. The Day of the Dead is a mixture of Aztec and Christian rituals in Mexican tradition. Death is not seen as an end in itself, but part of a continuous cycle. Traditions include making *ofrendas* (private family altars), sharing food, and performing publicly with music, masks, and puppets (Masuoka, 1994). Zarco extends the concept of family art into the community at large. Part of his family's performance includes skeleton masks and a giant puppet, representing Grandmother Death, *Dona Sebastiana*, made by Zarco (see Figure 6). He expresses disappointment when the Day of the Dead spectacle is used for profit and wants it to retain its more serious symbolic purpose. He organizes a group of Chicano artists for *"La Procesion Y Festival"* to honor those who have died, especially victims of violence. This annual procession involves several portable altars dedicated to all victims of violence, such as children, unborn babies, and women.

[2]Oral history, a story of everyday people, is the recording of someone's life story by a narrator. Its purpose is to document an individual and cultural heritage (Stokrocki, 1995).

[3]The ancient Aztecs believed the jaguar controlled rain. Every year in Acatlan, Mexico, they sacrificed someone to call forth rain for the growing season. Today men perform in jaguar costumes and masks, but when a player spills some blood on the ground, symbolizing fertility, the ritual ends (Amato, 1999).

[4]Carmen recently displayed her beadwork in the "Women of Color" exhibition during the Untold Stories Festival at Arizona State Univer-

sity, April 9-11, 1999. Zarco also performed in his new carved wooden mask series in a performance called "Face to Face."

References

Amato, M. (1999). The magic of masks. *Muse, 3* (4), 29-35.

Amparano, J. (1997, May 13). Mask maker to take work to stage. *Arizona Republic*, pp. A1, A6.

Bachelard, G. (1969). *The poetics of space.* Oxford: Oxford University Press.

Becker, H. (1982). *Art worlds.* Berkeley: University of California Press.

Cutting-Baker, H. (Ed.). (1976). *Family folklore.* Washington, D.C.: Smithsonian

D'Amico, V. (1954). *Art for the family.* New York: Simon and Schuster.

Huang, T. (1998, January 28). What pushes some at-risk kids to persevere? *The Arizona Republic*, p. C1 & C3.

Hyde, L. (1983). *The gift: Imagination and the erotic life of property.* New York: Random House.

Jones, D. (1959). *Epoch and artist.* London: Faber.

Lindgren, A. (1963). *The six Bullerby children.* London: Methuen.

Masuoka, S. (1994). *En calavera: The paper mache art of the Linares family.* Los Angeles: Fowler.

Mathiesen, E. (1982). Family art. In P. Pacey (Ed.), *Family art: Essays and a bibliography to accompany an exhibition* (pp. 5-6). Preston, UK: Preston Polytechnic.

Nesbit, E. (1913). *Wings and the child.* London: Hodder and Stoughton.

Pacey, P. (1989). *Family art.* Cambridge, MA: Basil Blackwell.

Silberstein-Storfer, M. (1982). *Doing art together: The remarkable parent-child workshop at the Museum of Modern Art.* New York: Simon & Shuster.

Slater, P. (1976). *The pursuit of loneliness: American culture at the breaking point.* Boston: Beacon.

Stokrocki, M. (1995). Oral history: Recording teaching folklore and folkways. In Peter Smith (Ed.). *Art Education historical methodology: An insider's guide to doing and using* (pp. 16-25). Monograph Series Sponsored by the Seminar for Research in Art Education. Pasadena, CA: Open Door.

chapter
⁖⚘⁖

17

The Ethnic Aesthetics of Pedro deLemos:
Editor, *The School Arts Magazine* (1919-1950)

John Howell White

Pedro J. deLemos

In 1919 the publishers of *The School Arts Magazine* selected Pedro J. Lemos[1] as editor to follow the legacy of its co-founder, Henry Turner Bailey. It was a decision that would affect the magazine and the field of art education for the following 30 years. Functionally, the selection marked a shift of editorial offices from New England to California. Historically, deLemos's tenure corresponded with an isolationist America's efforts to realign its relationship to the cultures from which its citizens had emigrated. Aesthetically, the move allowed art education's scope to include not only dominant Anglo-American art education culture but also Household Art[2] and multiethnic traditions, prefiguring the concerns of the late 20th century (White & Congdon, 1998).

The multiple contributions of deLemos to art education have yet to be fully appreciated. As well as serving as chief editor of *The School Arts Magazine* (1919-1950) for 31 years, he was Director of the Stanford University's Museum of Fine Arts (1917-1945), wrote 9 books, 51 portfolios, and hundreds of professional articles. He was a graphic artist who established a reputation in the California Arts and Crafts Movement and developed Spanish Colonial Revival architecture in Palo Alto, California.

Perhaps deLemos has been overlooked in the field of art education because his work was practical, not theoretical. Perhaps he has been overlooked because his prominence was generated by his own will, a force that can disappear at the end of a life. Perhaps art educators in the 1950s distanced themselves from genealogies of history and culture as they moved toward psychology and self-expression (White, 1997a).

The metaphoric perimeters of deLemos's art education includes an interplay between home and family as supportive ground and travel as expansive force. In private, deLemos manifested this synthesis through a search for his Hispanic ancestry. In public discourse of North American art education, Native American cultures provided a universal aesthetic homeland (family) for deLemos and other North American immigrants (travelers).

Grounding a Life: Family and Travel

DeLemos (1882-1954) was born in Austin, Nevada, and raised in Oakland, California. He was a graduate (1910) of the San Francisco Institute of Art, where he taught courses (1911-1917) in decorative design, normal art, and applied art. From teaching he moved rapidly into administration as the Director of the Institute (1913-1917), Director of Stanford University's Museum of Fine Art (1917-1945), and Editor of *The School Arts Magazine* (1919-1950).

DeLemos shared aesthetic values with the California Arts and Crafts Movement. Significant contributions to his aesthetic sensibilities can also be found in his Hispanic identity and his immigrant and working class background. He was increasingly driven to understand and appreciate the Folk and Household Arts of people from around the world, with a particular interest in Native American and Spanish cultures. Through *The School Arts Magazine*, these interests came to be shared by many art educators.

California's Mediterranean climate and diverse immigrant communities framed deLemos's life. His father, Francesco, immigrated from Spain to Berkeley in the early 1860s where he spent time as a rancher, moved to Nevada to mine for silver prior to 1868, and moved back to Oakland in 1883 where he made his living as a cobbler (personal correspondence of deLemos, 1947)[3].

Central to deLemos's aesthetic was his deep connection to family. The brothers, Frank, Pedro, and John, established an illustration and engraving business in 1905 that they moved to Oakland after the San Francisco fire of 1906. As the Director of Stanford's Museum of Fine Art, deLemos hired brother Frank as a permanent assistant and John as an occasional guard. John, a high school art teacher, wrote articles for *The School Arts Magazine* and served as its assistant editor during the 1920s. Eventually, deLemos's siblings and parents followed his move to Palo Alto.

DeLemos married Reta Bailey in 1907. They applied their shared interest in ornamental architectural handicrafts to a series of building projects in Palo Alto and Carmel, California; a book , *Color Cement Handicraft* (Lemos & Lemos, 1922); and to the documentation and collection of traditional works from many cultures.

The deLemos had three children, Margaret, Esther, and Marie. The three girls were introduced to art education through the editorial offices of *The School Arts Magazine*, which were housed in several Palo Alto locations while the children were growing up. Margaret and Esther both contributed illustrations, articles, and editorial expertise. Esther became the editor upon deLemos's retirement in 1950.

DeLemos's work with *The School Arts Magazine* was an exercise in community building. DeLemos and his family maintained an extended family relationship with his publisher's (Warren Davis) family. Together they traveled to the pueblos of the American Southwest. In advertisements and editorials, deLemos refers to his readers as *"The School Arts* family." The "family," a national community of art educators, was unified by the magazine's historical practice of publishing submissions from teachers in the field and deLemos's editorial policy that embraced the Household Art movement with its pragmatic connection between art and life. The magazine provided a forum for art education, a field that had not yet developed a national organization.

Throughout his career, deLemos made extended trips of several months each to Europe, Asia, and Central America, as well as frequent trips throughout the United States. His journeys began upon his graduation from college with a 1910 summer trip to New York City to study with Arthur Wessley Dow.[4]

The deLemos family in costume

Every trip that deLemos made provided an opportunity to synthesize his diverse interests in art, education, travel, and family. DeLemos and his wife made three European tours, in 1924, 1928, and 1934, all of which provided material for *The School Arts Magazine*.[5] For example, deLemos's sketches from the 1924 trip appeared in his *European Sketches* published by Binney and Smith (Lemos, 1925), *The School Arts Magazine*, and several Davis Publications' portfolios.

DeLemos saw travel as an opportunity to experience traditional cultures, Household Arts and people's lives. In a letter to subscribers with a boldfaced introductory exclamation, "I am making this art journey to Europe *for* YOU," deLemos (1928) speaks of the limits of traditional European tours:

> These pilgrimages have largely been made through itineraries organized by travel organizations who think of art in old term, in terms of painting and sculpture. Today the art teacher needs to find inspirational sources for the correlation of art in everyday life, for ideas in home building, in pageantry, in industrial design, in producing finer streets, better toys, artistic stagecraft, individual doorways, a finer sense of art principles that go toward producing more beauty and unity of life....I hope to find and describe and thereby create new points of interest for the art teacher who believes in progress and art ideas that are greater than only what may be found in the galleries and museums of Europe. (p. xxv)

Although deLemos saw Household Art as localized and traditional, his lived aesthetic explored a tension between home and travel.[6] Together these perspectives frame the aesthetic dimensions of his vision for the field of art education.

Genealogy: Surrogate and Genetic

In his 40 years in art education, deLemos's aesthetic posture moved from an abstract conception of pure design toward a grounded sensitivity based upon cultural context. DeLemos's development required this member of a minority culture to reconstruct and negotiate relationships between his familial, professional, and national identities. It is a change that is explicitly embodied in the 1943 publication of a bilin-

gual (Spanish-English) edition of *The School Arts Magazine* devoted
to traditional Latin American arts.

DeLemos's early aesthetic identity was influenced by two patriarchs of
art education—A. W. Dow and H. T. Bailey—and an aesthetic initiative, the Arts and Crafts Movement. He shared with these sources a
conception of design as symbolic of a well-ordered world. Califor-
nians who identified themselves with the Arts and Crafts Movement
were also fascinated by traditional Native American art and Spanish
Colonial architecture and furniture. Gustav Stickley's Mission Style
furniture was influenced by the Spanish colonial missions that extend
up the California coast. Although the Mission Style was accepted by
mainstream America, the politics of Hispanic identity was not. However, by 1920 Americans were ready to romantically value Native
American traditions. It was by way of this American reorientation
toward Native Americans that deLemos came to embrace a cultural
approach to art and, in turn, to claim his own ethnic heritage.

Native American art forms possessed several features valued by
deLemos, the Arts and Crafts Movement, and mainstream North
Americans. They were aboriginal American art forms. North Americans were simultaneously consolidating their American identity
through projects like the Panama Canal and removing themselves from
Europe, especially following World War I. Native American art also
exemplified principles of good design with its clear and simple features (Lemos, 1918). Native American pottery, in particular, was seen
as deeply connected to the daily lives of its makers and users (Lemos,
1923). As a surrogate or foster home culture, Native American art and
myths were appropriated as spiritual foster culture by America's more
recent immigrants (White, 1997b).

DeLemos's first published recognition of Native American cultures is a
broadly based call for appreciating indigenous, non-European art
(Lemos, 1918). There is little evidence that deLemos had yet helped to
form a community of people interested in Native American art. In the
summer of 1922, deLemos purchased Native American artifacts from
the American southwest for Stanford's Museum of Fine Arts, most
likely after a trip to the region. In *The Household Art of the Indian
Pueblos* deLemos reveals his philosophical interest in Native Ameri-

can pottery (Lemos, 1924). At an exhibition of Native American pottery at the Museum of New Mexico, deLemos was introduced to the work of Maria Martinez. Maria and her husband Julian were just beginning to emerge nationally as exemplary Native American artists. The exhibition's curator, Kenneth Chapman, took deLemos to the San Ildefonso pueblo to meet the Martinezes. As deLemos viewed Maria at work he stated:

> This work is truly a Household Art, as she produces this pottery aside from her work of grinding corn into meal and cooking and housekeeping, to say nothing of her small child who was blissfully asleep in a swing cradle hung from the rafters unconcerned with visitors. (p. 338)

The connections between art and life that deLemos saw in Maria Martinez's work corresponded with the values of Household Arts, the Arts and Crafts Movement, and deLemos's own connoisseurship.

The community of interest developing around southwestern Native American art and education intensified throughout the 1920s and 1930s. Since 1909, Chapman and Julian Martinez had been working with anthropologist Edgar Lee Hewitt[7] on a dig in Tuyuoni, New Mexico (Tremblay, 1994). Chapman served in various capacities for the Museum of New Mexico, the School of American Research, and the Laboratory of Anthropology, all in Santa Fe, NM. In 1922 Chapman co-founded the Indian Pottery Fund, designed to solicit donations of specimens of Indian pottery from private collections for the Museum of New Mexico. Those artworks were, in turn, to be used to educate Native Americans about their art:[8]

> From the very start the Fund has used every possible means of making its collection available to the Indians themselves. For those from the more remote villages and tribes, photographs and drawings , and duplicate specimens are provided and a similar service is being extended to the Government Indians Schools. (Chapman, 1931. p. 399)

Chapman, the Martinezes,[9] and deLemos were part of a broad national interest in reviving and preserving traditional Native American art forms. An editorial (*New York Herald Tribune*, 1927) mentions San Ildefonso, the School of American Research and the value of saving these art forms.

From 1919 - 1935 deLemos increased the number of Native American related articles in *The School Arts Magazine*, and his community of contributors and professional contacts expanded (White, 1997a). Articles submitted by art educators were increasingly grounded in specific Native American tribal artifacts and practices. Several submissions in the 1930s took strong political stands for maintaining tribal and historical identities (Peters, 1928; Horne, 1935). In the years between 1929 and 1945 the magazine became the dominant producer of Native American related educational materials (White, 1997a).

Zia Potter

Articles about Native American art education were also written. A central figure joining this developing community of interest is Dorothy Dunn. Dunn taught Native American children beginning in 1928. In 1933 she became the art teacher at the United States Indian School at Santa Fe where she was the teacher of Maria and Julian Martinez's son, Popovi Da (Rehnstrand, 1936). Dunn wrote articles for *The School Arts Magazine* (Dunn, 1931) and authored *American Indian painting of the southwest and plains areas* (Dunn, 1968) with a foreword written by Kenneth Chapman.

In the 1930s, deLemos made arrangements through two trading posts, owned by Berton Staples and Wick Miller, to exhibit the work of groups of Native Americans at Stanford University Museum of Fine Arts (Lemos, 1931a, 1931b).[10] The artists traveled to Stanford where they demonstrated their crafts and stayed as guests in the deLemos' Palo Alto, California home (Lemos, 1930).

Through these articles in *The School Arts Magazine* during the
deLemos years, art educators were invited to consider art in context
through approaches that were part ethnography, part travelogue, and
part advocacy. Artworks were simultaneously considered as aesthetic
objects, everyday tools, and symbols of ethnic identity. Many of these
articles provide more specifics about Native American traditions and
political positions than anything published in the magazine since
deLemos's retirement. For deLemos, they provided an opportunity to
understand ethnic identity from the outside, to travel to a readily
available culture, to conceptualize the authenticity of Household Art,
and romanticize an American identity. From there it was a short step
to engage in a search of his own household which included his, and
North America's, Hispanic ancestry.

It is not surprising that deLemos introduced art educators to America's
Hispanic identity through the Spanish missions that had been built in
the pueblo regions of the Southwest during the Spanish Colonial
Period (Vierra, 1924). Vierra provides a substantial history of the
missions, including the Native American influences on the New
Mexican style, influences that give that style a character substantially
different from their California and Central American counterparts.

Architecture is also the art form that deLemos used to integrate
Hispanic traditions into his own life. His first building project, designed with Reta deLemos, is the 1925 Studio Court Building at 520
Ramona St. in Palo Alto, California. The Studio Court building
became the editorial office of *The School Arts Magazine*, and also the
focus of an article in the magazine. The building served as a business
property that held, among other things, a shop for handicrafts run by
Reta (Lemos, 1927). As for the design, deLemos states,

> We have sought a common denominator in the decorations and we
> have used oriental motifs, Aztec and Mayan Indian, Pueblo and
> Spanish motifs in a way that no conflict is felt. California receives
> much oriental material, and with the Spanish period of occupation,
> together with the Indian traditions and handicrafts, we have used all
> of these as an influence in the design of Studio Court (p. 529)

This account downplays the Spanish Colonial design of this building, an influence which was to be embraced more completely in his next house.

His interest in his Spanish ancestry took on a greater urgency after the family's 1928 trip to Europe. DeLemos writes about the trip in a September 1929 issue of *The School Arts Magazine* devoted to Spain. His article is filled with sketches, photographs, and personal observations about Ronda, Spain (Lemos, 1929). It is clear that deLemos was captivated by the "unstaged beauty" of the everyday lives of the Spanish people. DeLemos altered his 1928 itinerary to include an extensive month of travel in western Spain and Portugal, his ancestral homeland.

It was probably this excursion that initiated his intensive personal search for information about the deLemos legacy in Spain and for evidence that would support a connection between his family and the aristocrat Conde (Count) de Lemos.[11] A letter (Hispanic Society of America, personal communication, June 2, 1932) addresses deLemos (then Pedro J. Lemos) as "Don Pedro J. de Lemos." The letter included title pages from two books by Miguel de Cervantes, author of Don Quixote. In Cervantes's last two books and *Don Quixote* (vol. 2, 2nd ed.), dating from the early 17th century, dedications from Cervantes to Conde deLemos are inscribed (deLemos, personal notes, n.d.).

In 1932, deLemos incorporated this dedication into a mural, *Cervantes in his Last Days Writes a Dedication to Conde de Lemos*, located at the Menlo Park, California, site of The Allied Arts Guild. The deLemos family, along with Garfield and Delight Merner, founded the guild in 1929 to educate and promote artists and ideas associated with the California Arts and Crafts Movement. DeLemos worked with architect Gardner Dailey on the Spanish Colonial Revival design of the building. California's Spanish ancestry was promoted through a series of mosaics executed by deLemos, with Reta, Margaret, and Esther. DeLemos's mural depicts Cervantes, on his death bed, writing a dedication to the Conde deLemos. The inscription reads, "Long live the great Conde de Lemos whose humanity and celebrated liberality without soliciting of adulation sustained me under the most severe blows of fortune."

Santa Fe Buildings

DeLemos returned to Spain in 1934 to settle an estate and reclaim "deLemos" as his rightful name. Immediately preceding this trip, an article, "Spanish Galicia: Switzerland of Spain" by Benton Court, appeared in *The School Arts Magazine* (Court, 1934). The article goes into great detail about the countryside and its history and makes specific reference to Cervantes and Monteforte deLemos, the 17th century hometown of the Conde de Lemos. It is a timely submission by Court who is listed as a "traveling artist and author." The article is prefaced with an illustration by deLemos. It is clear is that deLemos's ethnic identity and search achieved resolution around this time.

The most complete manifestation of his personal embrace of his Spanish heritage was the Hacienda deLemos, a 10 year project begun in 1931. The hacienda, which incorporated his home and *The School Arts Magazine's* office, was constructed with Spanish architectural and design influences and decorated with Spanish and Native American artifacts. True to deLemos's efficient and inclusive character, the design and decor of the Hacienda were shared with art educators in an insert for the May 1937 issue of the magazine (Lemos, 1937). Items in the hacienda referred to in the text included: the Toledo home of El Greco, a Spanish bell tower, a Romanesque Spanish sculpture, original hand-crafted 16th and 17th century iron window grills, doors from a 16th century church in Ronda, Spain, decorative Spanish nail heads, and medieval Spanish door knockers, all ideas and artifacts obtained during his trips to Europe. La Hacienda becomes deLemos's Hispanic sanctuary in California.

In the New World, deLemos's moral sympathies were with the Native American populations displaced by the Spanish and with the Spanish displaced by the United States. Central America became a region within which he could balance out Hispanic-Indian relationships. This is stated clearly in the January 1938 issue of *The School Arts Magazine*, which is devoted to Mexico. DeLemos's (1938) lead editorial states:

> The history of Mexico is one of strife and struggle between ART and GOLD....One represents BEAUTY and the other represents GREED....Down the ages a war has almost constantly waged between these two factions in the land of the Aztecs and, briefly told, its history can be summed in Gold-Cortez-Conquest, Mines-United States-invasion, Oil-Corporations-Control....Today we find the Indian justly coming into possession of his country in Mexico. Tenaciously their art has survived. (p. 130)

The complexity and significance of the Spanish influence on Native American art is developed in his 1933 article "Santa Fe, Ancient Spanish Art Center," which is rich in content and strongly affirmative of Spanish colonial influences (Lemos, 1933). He states:

> Later it was decided to send from Mexico, weavers skilled in their art, so that industry might be introduced and so that it could progress in the new country....Today the village of Chimayo, north of Santa Fe, home of the famous Chimayo blanket, is considered a survival of the art of these early craftsmen. (pp. 332, 334)

America's Hispanic identity is interwoven with the identities of Native American peoples, especially in Mexico, Central America, and the American southwest.

DeLemos's interest in Hispanic and Native American art brought him a commission by the Mexican government in 1931 to conduct a survey of Mexican Arts and Crafts. True to his entrepreneurial and inclusive instincts, he devoted the February 1932 issue of *The School Arts Magazine* to Mexico. It includes an article by Diego Rivera on children's art, a painting by Frida Kahlo, an article by Rene D'Harnoncourt, future director of the Museum of Modern Art, on Mexican toys, and an article by Juan Olaguibel, Head of the Department of Fine Art for Mexico's Ministry of Public Education, on drawing in Mexico's public schools. In *Guatemala Art Crafts* (Lemos, 1941), deLemos praises the connection between art and life that exists there and attributes it to the Spanish restraint in allowing the native populations to continue their craft.

In April, 1942 we see the culmination of deLemos's journey, the first and only bilingual edition of *The School Arts Magazine* entitled "Pan American Travels." This edition presages the bilingual education movement by 30 years. True to deLemos's community-as-family model, brother Frank is on the Spanish editorial staff, listed as "Francesco B. deLemos." The issue was organized in co-operation with the Pan American Union in Washington, DC, probably as a symbol of solidarity in World War II. The issue contains articles related to the arts and crafts of Spain, Guatemala, Bolivia, Costa Rica, Uruguay, Ecuador, Peru, Columbia, Mexico, Los Angeles, Argentina, and Panama.

The tension between the public and private dimensions of deLemos's aesthetic search was a powerful force that encompassed a complex set of people, practices, and artifacts. These included his immediate family, *The School Arts Magazine*'s readers, authors, and owners; Native American artists, students, artifacts, and customs; the residents and workers of Palo Alto, California; Stanford University's faculty and Museum of Fine Arts with its collection, patrons, and museum visitors; and the international communities that deLemos visited. Art education was immensely affected by these relationships. The life and work of Pedro deLemos serves as an allegory for American art education's development. The aesthetic journey that began with an Anglo-Ameri-can call for hierarchies of design, beauty and industrious work ended with a respect for the complexity of lived personal (family) and public (travel) worlds. DeLemos's journey serves as a historical reference for contemporary art educators who value an aesthetic that maps diverse and often conflicting cultural, biological, familial and institu-tional contexts. This aesthetic is one of development and flux in that its pervasive quality involves a capacity to experience and value the partiality and blending of those distinct cultural and personal contexts that surround and inhabit us.

Author's Note

The author would like to thank Phyllis Lyon Munsey, granddaughter of Pedro J. deLemos, for granting me access to family archives, Eldon Katter for access to past issues of *The School Arts Magazine*, and Kathryn E. Hood for editorial comments. Much of the research for this chapter included unpublished primary sources such as personal correspondences, office documents, photographs, film footage, and travel documents. As often as possible, multiple sources were sought for verification.

Endnotes

[1]In 1934 Pedro Lemos reverted to his Spanish family name "deLemos." Much of his professional work is listed under "Lemos." "DeLemos" is used throughout this text except in relation to reference sources.
[2]Household Arts was an art educational initiative that took place in the first quarter of this century. It stressed connections between art and life.
[3]This account is taken from a letter deLemos wrote in 1947. There are conflicting accounts of this family history but this is the most original source I have located.
[4]Dow influenced art education's adoption of the elements and principles of design as a unifying set of first principles. DeLemos's prints, illustrations, and teaching methods show his influence.
[5]The whole family traveled together on the 1924 and 1928 tours.
[6]If Household Arts and the values that they embody were aesthetically fulfilling for deLemos, he may have chosen to stay home and explore a very personal and local world. Of course he then would have been a very different person.
[7]Edgar Lee Hewitt was a motivating force behind the formation of the Museum of New Mexico. He served as its Director from 1909-1917 (Kardon, 1994).
[8]The archeologist-as-colonialist implications here are worth reflecting upon. Archeologists, such as Hewitt, felt that traditions related to pottery design and construction were in danger of being lost (Chapman, 1953). Questions about ownership of these art forms and the means by which they, as cultural knowledge, were disseminated are important post colonial issues. The Pottery Fund itself was used to buy up post-Spanish colonial ceramics from Native American owners (Chapman, 1953) causing a depletion of these wares in the everyday lives of the pueblo peoples.
[9]The Martinezes relation to European culture, creativity, and appropriation are much more complex that this account implies. Their use of traditional, Native American design is layered with an understanding of Art Deco. For a discussion see Tremblay, 1994.

[10]Miller not only organized this group for Stanford but later arranged for regular traveling commercial exhibitions of Native Americans and their art titled *Exhibit of Indian Craftsmen at Work* in national department stores such as Joseph Horne in Pittsburgh, The Emporium in San Francisco, and F & R Lazarus & Co. in Chicago. Miller (personal communication to Pedro, August 7, 1932) credits Pedro as the founder of the idea.

[11]Personal correspondences indicate that deLemos researched his genealogy in Madrid on this trip.

References

Cervantes, Miguel de, *Don Quixote* (Vol. 2, 2nd ed.).

Chapman, K. (1931, March). America's most ancient art. *The School Arts Magazine, 30* (7) 387-402.

Chapman, K. (1953). *The pottery of the Santo Domingo pueblo.* Santa Fe: Laboratory of Anthropology.

Court, B. (1934). Spanish Galicia: The Switzerland of Spain. *The School Arts Magazine, 33* (7) 386-400.

Dunn, D. (1931, March). Going to school with little Domingos. *The School Arts Magazine, 30* (7) 469-480.

Dunn, D. (1968). *American Indian painting of the southwest and plains areas.* Albuquerque: University of New Mexico Press.

Horne, E. (1935, October). Preserve Indian culture. *The School Arts Magazine, 35* (2) 72-75.

Kardon, J. (1994). *Revivals! Devours traditions.* New York: Abrams.

Lemos, P.J. (1918, September). Are you an Assyrian? *The School Arts Magazine, 18* (1) 16-18.

Lemos, P.J. (1923).

Lemos, P.J. (1924, February). The Household Arts of the Indian pueblos. *The School Arts Magazine, 23* (6), 334-341.

Lemos, P.J. (1925). *European sketches.* Binney and Smith: New York.

Lemos, P.J. (1927, May). A tree covered business home. *The School Arts Magazine, 26* (9), 523-529.

Lemos, P.J. (1928, May). From Pedro J. Lemos. *The School Arts Magazine, 27* (9) xxv.

Lemos, P.J. (1929, September). Art rambles: Ronda, the bridge town of Spain. *The School Arts Magazine, 29* (1), 3-13.

Lemos, P.J. (1930, June). My five Indian guests, each one an artist. *The School Arts Magazine, 29* (10), 589-601.

Lemos, P.J. (1931a, March). Crafts del Navajo: A unique Navajo trading post. *The School Arts Magazine, 30* (7), 454-455.

Lemos, P.J. (1931b, March). Wick Miller, friendly Indian trader, and his post for pueblo Indians. *The School Arts Magazine, 30* (7), 467-468.

Lemos, P.J. (Ed.). (1932, February). Mexico [Special Issue]. *The School Arts Magazine, 31* (6).

Lemos, P.J. (1933, February). Santa Fe, ancient Spanish art center. *The School Arts Magazine, 32* (6), 327-254.

Lemos, P.J. (1937, May). Thirty years of progress in art education. *The School Arts Magazine, 36* (9), supplement.

Lemos, P.J. (1938, January). Art and gold. *The School Arts Magazine, 37* (5), 130.

Lemos, P.J. (1941). *Guatemala art crafts.* Worchester, MA: Davis Publications.

Lemos, P.J. (Ed.). (1942, April). Pan American travels [Special Issue]. *The School Arts Magazine, 41* (8).

Lemos, P.J. & Lemos, R. (1922). *Color Cement Handicraft.* Worchester, MA: Davis Publications.

New York Herald-Tribune (1927, November). Indian Crafts: Reviving a lost art. *The School Arts Magazine, 27* (3) 192a.

Peters, S. (1928, December). An appeal from the first American craftsmen. *The School Arts Magazine, 28* (4) 218.

Rehnstrand, J. (1936). Young Indians revive their art. *The School Arts Magazine, 36* (3) 137-143.

Tremblay, G. (1994). Cultural survival and innovation: Native American aesthetics. In Kardon, J. (Ed.), *Revivals! Devours traditions.* New York: Abrams.

Vierra, C. (1924, November). Some early American art. *The School Arts Magazine, 24* (3) 131.

White, J.H. (1997a). Intersection: *School Arts Magazine* and Native American culture. In P. Bolin & A. Anderson (Eds.), *History of Art Education* (pp. 95-104). The Pennsylvania State University.

White, J.H. (1997b, September). Jaune Quick-to-See Smith: Give back. *School Arts, 97* (2), 27-30.

White, J.H. & Congdon, K.G. (1998). Travel, boundaries, and the movement of culture(s): Explanations for the folk/fine art quandary. *Art Education, 51* (3), 21-42.

Left to right; Boldin, Congdon, Blandy

About the Editors

Kristin G. Congdon

Kristin G. Congdon has taught art in a variety of settings, including public schools, correctional settings, treatment facilities, museums, and universities. She has a PhD in art education from the University of Oregon and has published extensively on the study of folk arts, community arts, and contemporary art issues.

She is co-editor, with Doug Blandy, of *Art in a Democracy* (Teachers College Press, 1987) and *Pluralistic Approaches to Art Criticism* (Popular Press, 1991). With Doug Boughton she co-edited *Evaluating Art Education Programs in Community Centers: International Perspectives on Problems of Conception and Practice* (JAI, 1998) and with Paul Bolin and Doug Blandy she co-edited *Remembering Others: Making Invisible Histories of Art Education Visible* (NAEA, 2000). Additionally, she has two authored books scheduled for publication. They are: *Uncle Monday and Other Traditional Tales from Florida* (University of Mississippi

Press) and *Community-Based Art Programming* (Davis). She is the 1988 and 1999 recipient of the Manuel Barkan Memorial Award for scholarship from the National Art Education Association and the 1998 Ziegfeld Award from the United States Society for Education Through Art for international work in the arts.

Dr. Congdon is a recent President of the Florida Folklore Society, a member of the Florida Folklife Council, and a member of the National Planning Committee for the Zora Neale Hurston Festival of the Arts and Humanities. She is a Professor of Art and Philosophy at the University of Central Florida.

Doug Blandy

Doug Blandy's studies in Art Education at Ohio University (BS, 1974) and The Ohio State University (MA, 1979; PhD, 1983); his association with schools, community arts centers, and universities; and his research has attended to providing art educational experiences that meet the needs of students within a lifelong learning context. Research and teaching also attends to the relationships between art, education, community, and place.

Dr. Blandy's research has been published in *Studies in Art Education, Art Education,* the *Journal of Multicultural and Cross-Cultural Research in Art Education,* and the *Visual Sociology Review,* among other journals. He co-edited with Kristin G. Congdon *Art in a Democracy* and *Pluralistic Approaches to Art Criticism.* With Paul Bolin and Kristin G. Congdon he co-edited *Remembering Others: Making Invisible Histories of Art Education Visible.*

Dr. Blandy's research, teaching and service has been recognized with the 1997 Mary J. Rouse Award, 1992 NAEA Manuel Barkan Research Award, and delivery of a Kenneth Marantz Invited Lecture at The Ohio State University in 1993.

Dr. Blandy is currently the Director of the University of Oregon's Arts and Administration Program and Institute for Community Arts Studies.

Paul E. Bolin

Paul E. Bolin is an Associate Professor of Art Education and Head of the Art Education Program at The Pennsylvania State University. He received is graduate degrees (MS, 1980; PhD, 1986) in Art Education from the University of Oregon, after completing his undergraduate degree (BA, 1976) at Seattle Pacific University.

Dr. Bolin's research interests center around historical issues in art education , particularly within the context of late nineteenth century public schools and schooling in the United States. His research and teaching also focus on relationships that occur between people and objects, with particular interest in the field of material culture studies.

His work has been published in *Studies in Art Education, Art Education, Journal of Social Theory in Art Education*, and *Arts and Learning Research*, among other journals. In 1997, Dr. Bolin received the Manuel Barkan Memorial Award, from the National Art Education Association, in recognition of his published work. In 2000, Dr. Bolin co-edited with Doug Blandy and Kristin Congdon *Remembering Others: Making Invisible Histories of Art Education Visible*. Dr. Bolin recently completed his term as Editor of *Art Education*, the journal of the National Art Education Association.

Contributors

Faith Agostinone-Wilson is an adjunct instructor at Park College where she teaches courses in curriculum and instruction and popular culture. She also teaches art in a local retirement community.

Alice Arnold is an Associate Professor of Art Education at East Carolina University in Greenville, North Carolina. Her research has focused on interdisciplinary methods of instruction in the visual and performing arts.

June Elizabeth Eyestone Finnegan is an Associate Professor of Art Education at Florida State University where she teaches courses in art and museum education. She has published articles on the history of art education and early childhood education in art.

Charles R. Garoian is the Director of the School of Visual Arts at the Pennsylvania State University, and author *of Performing Pedagogy: Toward an Art of Politics* published by The State University of New York Press.

Karen Kakas teaches art education classes at Bowling Green State University in Bowling Green, Ohio.

Kathleen Keys is the Curator and Manager of the Ohio State University-Newark Gallery. Her research and professional interests include arts organizations and their roles in society, and critical analyses of art exhibitions.

Hyungsook Kim is a PhD candidate at the Ohio State University. She has written on postmodern art criticism and organized several art exhibitions in Korea.

Jean Ellen Jones is Associate Director and Associate Professor of Art Education in the School of Art and Design, Georgia State University in Atlanta. She has published descriptive studies about adults in community art settings and articles connecting motivation theory to art education.

Stanley Madeja is a Professor of Art and Chair of the Art Education Division of the School of Art, Northern Illinois University.

Paula L. McNeill is an Assistant Professor of Art at Valdosta State University in Valdosta, Georgia, where she teaches art education, art criticism, and aesthetics. Her current research interest is the history of photography in art education. While in Georgia, she has also been documenting and utilizing folk art from the area in her university classes.

Melody Milbrandt is an Assistant Professor at the State University of West Georgia where she teaches courses in art education. Her research and publications have focused on the importance of addressing postmodern concerns through contemporary art education.

Christine Ballengee Morris is an Assistant Professor at the Ohio State University-Newark where she teaches art education and art classes. She explores multicultural, cross-cultural, and inter-cultural issues and arts-centered integrated approaches in the classroom.

Milda Baksys Richardson is a doctoral candidate in the Art History Department at Boston University. Her current research relates to ecclesiastical architecture and Lithuanian religious folk art.

Mary Stokrocki is a Professor at Arizona State University where she teaches aesthetics and art criticism as well as other art education classes. She has written extensively on teaching and learning in the schools in the United States, Turkey, Brazil, and Croatia.

John Howell White is an Associate Professor at Kutztown University where he teaches courses in curriculum and aesthetics. He has written about the history of art education and pragmatic aesthetics.

Barbara Fleisher Zucker an independent scholar and consultant, has taught in the university setting and in elementary schools where many of her students have been disabled. She has published widely on print and nonprint media and the museum.